Living With Max

Living With Max

Sandy Lewis

Vermilion
LONDON

1 3 5 7 9 10 8 6 4 2

Published in 2008 by Vermilion, an imprint of Ebury Publishing

A Random House Group Company

The Random House Group Limited Reg. No. 954009

Addresses for companies within the Random House Group can be
found at www.randomhouse.co.uk

A CIP catalogue record for this book is available from
the British Library

The Random House Group Limited supports The Forest
Stewardship Council (FSC), the leading international forest
certification organisation. All our titles that are printed on
Greenpeace approved FSC certified paper carry the FSC logo.
Our paper procurement policy can be found at
www.rbooks.co.uk/environment

Mixed Sources

Product group from well-managed
forests and other controlled sources
www.fsc.org Cert no. TT-COC-2139
© 1996 Forest Stewardship Council

Printed and bound in Great Britain by
Mackays of Chatham plc, Chatham, Kent

ISBN 9780091922085

To buy books by your favourite authors and register for offers
visit www.rbooks.co.uk

For
Paul, Max and Charlie, my loves, my life

Foreword

When we started filming *Notes on a Scandal* in the late summer of 2005, Max's father, Paul, asked me rather diffidently if he could say something about the script. 'Just one line,' he said. 'You would never say that a child *was* Down's syndrome, you'd say he *had* Down's syndrome.' And the more that I came to know Max, the more I understood what he was saying: that to describe Max (or any child) as simply the sum of his debilitating condition was to reduce him to a helpless victim and, as I shortly discovered with Max, nothing could be further from the truth.

Max is a gifted actor and a true professional. He always knew the distinction between himself and the character he was playing, Ben. And even if there were similarities between the two – a fondness for food, for football (West Ham) and for dancing – he was fastidious about the script's demands on his being 'Ben' and the obligation to repeat actions and lines from take to take, from set up to set up, sometimes over a period of several hours.

It's true that he could be difficult – there were times when he was unwilling to do another take and there were times when his demands were, well, imperious ('No fireworks!' he said on one occasion), but no more so than most film stars, none of whom are redeemed by the sweetness of nature and the goodwill that Max possesses. Anyone who has met Max will know that I'm not patronising him. To know him at all is to be capsized by his intelligence and by his mature sense of *self*: he knows who he is.

That I am writing about Max in this way – or indeed at all – is a refutation of the doctors' dismal predictions at his birth. If they have been proved wrong, it's as much his parents' triumph as it is Max's. It's Sandy and Paul's unquenchable faith that has given him the confidence to realise his remarkable self. Thanks to them for letting me work with Max, but above all thanks – and love – to Max.

Richard Eyre, 2008

7 September 2005

It's blisteringly hot; there's been no rain for over a week, so the street looks parched. Max and I are perched on the steps of a large Georgian house in Belsize Park. The cast and crew from Notes on a Scandal *are taking a break from filming. Max and I could retire to a cute little flat in the basement especially set aside for him, but he prefers to be in the thick of it. So here we sit, munching on doughnuts whilst being entertained by Bill Nighy as he enthusiastically recounts a tale about his favourite icon, Bob Dylan.*

In the flesh Bill, who plays Ben's Dad, is surprisingly animated and flirtatious, unlike his onscreen characters who are usually so bohemian and cool. Cate Blanchett is on the next step down from Max and me, shockingly beautiful and refreshingly down to earth. Judi Dench is finding solace in the shade; she's resting her dodgy knee and goes over her lines, still in character. Although the atmosphere is relaxed and friendly, it still feels odd to me that we're here.

In the film, which deals with jealousy and deceit and demonstrates how we can cause havoc to those we love, Max plays a boy called Ben who has Down's syndrome. Max also has Down's syndrome, but that's not why he got the part. During his audition, Max blew away both the director, Sir Richard Eyre, and the casting director, Maggie Lunn. He tends to do that; he knocks people off their feet. Putting aside the fact I am his proud mother, I've seen first hand how he lights up when a camera captures his face, how he moves with a quality that connects with – and enthrals – an audience. He can act when directed, but on a day-to-day level he performs to the world at every given opportunity. Max is happiest when he knows he's grabbed an audience. And that is great. But, of course, it's not the whole story.

Chapter One

I feel hesitant, almost ashamed, to speak the whole truth about having Max in our lives. Make no mistake: we have had many luminous, wonderful moments. But at the same time, we've all been on a tough, unrelenting journey where there are no maps to guide us, and wherever we go people always look at us with pity.

Everyone says that having children brings out emotions in you that you didn't know you had. Having a child with special needs brings out emotions in you that you're not even sure you *should* be having. Part of the reason is that you don't ever expect to be a statistic. It's always other people who fall foul of the odds, the ones you read about and feel sorry for. Before I had Max, our first child, I was like that. I'd had a pretty good life, free from any real adversity or hardship, and had no reason to believe that it wouldn't continue to yield any more than the usual trials that come with the territory. As an insolvency administrator I suppose I should have considered that, like investments, life can go up or down without warning. In my world that only happened on paper. I cared for the people I loved, tried to respect those I didn't and felt I was doing my best. I was 29 years old, married to a wonderful man and life was about as good as it got.

It was Tuesday 9 March 1993. That day, waiting on the steps leading up to the maternity unit of St Mary's Hospital in Paddington, I didn't feel right. The fact that I was sitting on a towel because I was dribbling amniotic fluid didn't help; for the first time in my life, I felt I had very little control over my destiny. Paul, my husband, was somewhere in the middle of London's lunchtime madness trying to park the car and I wished to God he'd hurry up. My anxiety was starting to get the better of me. I started crying but nobody seemed to notice or, if they did, showed absolutely no interest at all. After all, to this hospital I was just another one of the thousands of women who have babies every day. Paul was soon by my side, carrying a ridiculous amount of baggage. On reflection we must have looked liked first-time package tourists to Malaga – those people who feel that if they don't bring it with them the locals won't have it. We'd packed energy tablets, aromatherapy oils, calming music and a camera. We were prepared for any eventuality, or so we thought. We desperately scanned the corridor for someone who might rescue us until finally a very tired-looking nurse appeared. She looked at me and produced a form.

'Why are you crying?'

'Oh, I'm just scared of what's going to happen. You know, the pain ...'

She didn't react but passed the form to me to complete, glancing with irritation at our pile of luggage.

'How far apart are your contractions?'

'Well I haven't actually had any yet. My waters have broken. It happened this morning at about eight, and I rang here. I was told to have a bath and to come in, take my time, but to come ...'

'Well, we've no room for you. You shouldn't have come.'

No room at the inn. Well that's that then. I wasn't really sure what I was supposed to say or do next.

Towards the latter part of my pregnancy I remember being at home listening to Radio 4. A programme about people with Down's syndrome came on and I had to turn off the radio. Other pregnant women I met would gleefully complain about being kept awake all night because their bundle of joy was thrashing about inside them. Max, however, hardly ever moved. He moved enough for me to know that he wasn't dead, but perhaps only once or twice a day. It was as if he was making just enough movement to tell me he was there, but no more than that. If I thought about it too often a sickening, anxious feeling would seep into me. I tried to block it out of my head and I certainly never voiced my concerns to anyone; after all, that would have made them real. Perhaps the thought of my quiet, still baby was in my subconscious throughout my labour? Perhaps it was that the gas and air cylinder I was initially connected to was empty, setting off my deep anxiety and causing me to plead with the hospital staff to let me go home? Whatever it was, for years afterwards I would relive the moments of Max's birth with great distress.

Although he came out fast, the birth of Max Oliver Sinclare Lewis was not especially dramatic or difficult. Once he was delivered a pause settled over the room bringing with it a sense of relative calm. Max was strangely quiet; there was no loud wail to signal his entry into the world. The midwife passed him up to me and as I looked at his beautiful face I knew immediately.

'Does he have Down's syndrome?'

'What are you talking about?' The midwife seemed unprepared for the question.

'Does he have Down's syndrome?' I repeated. By now the question was redundant because I was absolutely certain that he did have it.

Perhaps it was the terse directness of my manner but the midwife didn't seem to be taking the question on board.

'Well, I don't think so, but I'll get the paediatrician. You're in shock. What you need is a cup of tea, love. Let's wait to see what the doctor says.'

Everyone suddenly became very busy, fetching refreshments and filling in the necessary paperwork that comes with having a baby. Paul and I took turns to cuddle Max as we sipped our tea, and for a moment we were in that blissful parental state that the books tell you about. Meanwhile, Max's sudden entrance into the world meant that I needed a considerable amount of stitches. I was told someone would arrive in a few hours to fix me up. I have absolutely no recollection of what transpired during that time but I do know that I felt very frightened. The staff obviously suspected that I was a long way from being okay, mentally as well as physically, but nobody was saying too much. Shortly after my stitches were completed, I was taken to a room of my own, rather than the normal post-natal ward. Paul and I wondered about this but we left the matter unchallenged. To be honest we were both so confused and exhausted we were grateful for the privacy.

A short time later – it must have been about 2.30 in the morning – a doctor arrived to talk with me. She performed a thorough examination on Max: he had not scored well on his Apgar birth test. This is a test that evaluates newborns on a scale of 1–10 measuring activity, pulse, grimace, appearance and respiration. It was clear that he had talipes, also known as club foot, in both feet. His feet were turned inwards and rested at an odd angle. The doctor suggested that it could have been how he had laid in the womb and said it was unfortunate, but fixable. She also remarked at how lovely and pink he was, which she felt was a good sign and suggested he didn't have the heart problems that afflict many babies born with Down's syndrome. But then her tone changed and she started talking about people with Down's being very loving and good at music. She mentioned the Special Olympics and I could tell she was struggling. By now I was certain that she knew what Max had, but I wanted her to acknowledge my fears.

'Please tell me. Do you think my baby has Down's syndrome?'

Averting her gaze the doctor paused, nervously shuffling her files, and then seemed to accept she had no option but to voice what I already knew to be true.

'We have to do a blood test to be sure and I do so hope that I'm wrong, but yes, I do think that he has Down's syndrome.'

I welcomed her honesty but even though this was what I had known all along, the confirmation of Max's condition felt like a knife slicing through all my precious hopes and dreams. I began to cry and once I started I couldn't stop; the tears just flooded out. As the doctor left the room I was still crying. Apart from knowing that my baby had a serious genetic defect, I was completely unaware how this defect would manifest in Max. Other than a vaguely superficial understanding, I had no knowledge about Down's syndrome (DS). All the stereotypical horrors came flooding into my mind. I had visions of short, stout people with their tongues protruding from their vacant faces, as they peered from Variety Club buses, en route to or from some cold, grey, charitable institution. I was already obsessing over whether Max would be able to go to the toilet unaided or if he would need to wear a nappy all his life. With all of this swirling around in my head, I persuaded Paul to go home and get some rest. God knows he was going to need it.

Although it was the middle of the night I called my parents. I was greeted with the reassuring voice of my mother who cheerfully assumed I just wanted to chat. I told her that it was almost certain that Max had DS. She may have been alarmed but she never let on. I know she bravely kept the tone of her voice light and breezy – but I have no idea what she said. It was as if I was in a different, parallel universe to her. I then rang Paul who, needless to say, was not asleep. We had one of those conversations that you have very rarely in your life, spoke to each other in a way that only comes when something has seriously upset your equilibrium. I wanted Paul to know how protective I felt about Max and how much I loved him, warts and all. I was passionate about him, about the journey we were about to undertake. It probably didn't need saying but I felt I had to put my feelings into words for Paul. Thankfully his feelings mirrored mine.

I didn't sleep at all that night. The shock to both my body and brain was so intense and it felt like raw emotions were bleeding through to the surface of my skin.

Just as dawn broke I had a visitor. It was Ruth, the midwife who'd delivered Max. She was to be the first of many diamonds to drop into the palm of my hand. Ruth brought me a cup of tea and sat with me. She didn't have to; it was the end of her night shift and I'm sure there were people waiting for her but, instead, she showed me a tremendous kindness that I shall never forget. How easy it would have been for her to say the usual clichés and head home. She could have simply brushed aside the fact that Max was the first child she had ever delivered with DS, but she didn't. Throughout my entire stay in hospital she visited me every day, and continued to come to our flat in Kilburn for months afterwards.

A few hours after Ruth left, a nurse came to tell me there was a man at reception saying he was my father. It *was* my father; he commuted daily to London from Bath. Unable to sleep following my phone call, he'd caught an early train and was to be the first person from our family and friends to meet Max. I'd love to say it was a happy moment but it was terribly sad. I desperately wanted to believe that now my dad was here, he would fix everything for me. He has an aura about him of calm and peace and just hearing his voice or being in his company never fails to fill me with an inner tranquillity. This tower of strength had ensured I'd had a secure, loving childhood so surely he could do something, couldn't he? I remember the tears falling from my face as I asked what on earth I'd done to deserve such a cruel twist of fate. He had no answers and never attempted to provide any. Only now can I imagine how that moment must have felt to him as a parent. Being powerless to help your own child must have been devastating. Yet there he stood, elegant and dignified in his grey pinstriped suit, smiling as he held little Max, who was dressed in a fuchsia pink babygro. I knew Dad was deeply moved and upset, but he left me with more smiles and a hug.

Next to arrive was a drawn and weary Paul. He wrapped me in an embrace that, to this day, has never faltered. Paul stayed with Max while I had a bath. I returned to find a nurse attempting to extract blood from my baby's tiny heel so they could test for DS. Max didn't cry but part of me wished that he would. At least then I would have some sign that he was like other children.

Shortly afterwards my mum arrived and I could see she adored Max straight away, which made me feel better. He was adorable, but despite my mother's affection for my son, I didn't feel that I could truly delight in him. One reason for this was my own worry that I'd produced faulty goods. I was also silenced by the reactions I'd received from some of the hospital staff. In any case, the idea of demonstrating any sort of joy seemed completely out of place. Our little room soon became a junction where strangers came and went, some wordlessly. In the middle of it all was me. Wearing my nightdress, clutching Max, feeling utterly pathetic and lost.

The blood test confirmed what we already knew.

Max had Down's syndrome. One in every thousand babies born will have DS, a genetic condition. People with DS have an extra chromosome. Instead of the usual 46 chromosomes in the cells of their body, there is an extra chromosome 21, making 47 in all. No one knows for sure why a child is born with DS. It is not because the mother drank or smoked during pregnancy or because the mother necessarily did anything before, during or after conception, although the production of the extra chromosome that produces DS happens at the very moment of conception. It's not something that necessarily runs in families, although you'd be forgiven for being nervous about your offspring if your cousin, uncle or sister were to have a baby with DS. There is certainly no known way to prevent it.

The doctors spoke to me in a cool, clinical and what I now know to be an ill-informed fashion. I don't think I absorbed much. I didn't want to. They would say things like 'when he's older, if you're really lucky, he might be able to go to the shops to buy a punnet of strawberries', but they had no way of knowing exactly what the future held in store for my son. I asked if he would be incontinent. They said they couldn't be sure, which scared the hell out of me. Today I know many people with DS and they are all perfectly capable of going to the toilet on their own.

These people – these 'authorities' – seemed ill-equipped for explaining the condition to parents who might have understandable fears and anxieties about the future of a child with a diagnosis of Down's syndrome. Because of what I now believe was a huge gap in their experience of people with DS, these doctors were unable to provide us with any support in dealing with our terrifying road ahead.

Once the results of the blood tests came through, a bureaucratic machine swung into action as people arrived to fill forms and take measurements. It was all so practical. Where was the emotional understanding and support that we so desperately needed? I didn't want pity but I would have liked some empathy. The same day Max was sent for a heart scan, and again it was all so cold and impersonal. He lay across my lap as a paediatric cardiologist scanned his heart. Nothing was said for the entire time. The doctor never explained what he was doing or gave Paul and me any reassurances. And then there was the noise: it was terrifying, with every heartbeat magnified to a frightening sound level. When the doctor completed his examination of Max we were told he had a hole in his heart. Not the typical hole seen in babies with DS but another type. He said it was big but it could very possibly heal itself. We would have to see, but in the meantime we would be referred to another cardiologist. At that point I realised that this is what my life would become, Max and I being passed from one doctor to another.

Chapter Two

11 January

Went for my daily run today. It actually always works out to be every other day, for which I'm plagued with guilt. I guess I just have to hold on to my best intentions. I pace the streets for three miles, passing a hospice about halfway. Before I turn and head for home, I indulge in my ritual of patting a particular bollard on the pavement. Once or twice a week I pass a guy in an electric wheelchair who is making the short journey from the hospice to the shops. Even though he's sitting down I can tell he's tall and thin and I'd put him in his early seventies. He's so cheeky and flirtatious and I'm sure he must have been a handful as a child and a nightmare as a teenager. I shoot him a massive smile. He blows me kisses and cheers and we do a high five, though I never stop. He's so full of life; he's itching to jump out of the chair and

*join me, even though we both know he can't. It
weighs on me that this man would give anything to
be walking, never mind running like me, and I
chastise myself that it takes all my determination
to get out there every day. He hasn't been around
these last few weeks, and I know what that means.
I miss him; I miss him reminding me that
everything is relative.*

Having a child is supposed to symbolise the renewal of life but with Max there was always the possibility of an infection or a complication with the hole in his heart that could possibly be fatal. Babies who have Down's syndrome are also more susceptible to respiratory problems and gastrointestinal disorders than children born without the condition. I would be constantly checking him for warning signs, telling myself that he was fine for today and crossing my fingers that a potentially life-threatening illness wouldn't occur this week or even this year. Every day, from the moment I awoke, until the moment I went to sleep, I would find it hard to shake the thought that I would almost certainly outlive my child. That's not me being dramatic, that's just the reality of having a child with DS.

Twenty-four hours after Max's birth, my natural

survival instinct began to kick in and so did my readiness to protect my son against the world. Perhaps this sounds adversarial but it's just the way I felt at that moment. The general reaction we'd had from the hospital not only made us feel isolated and uncomfortable, it also meant we didn't really enjoy our son. We desperately wanted permission to celebrate this little chubby-faced baby, but instead we felt like we should stay quiet. Sitting in that hospital we realised this was going to be something we would have to fight for all our lives, all of Max's life. The preconceptions and prejudices of so-called 'normal' society is and will always be Max's biggest obstacle to overcome.

Added to the poor attitude of some of the nursing staff, and my own emotional upheaval as I was getting my head around what it meant not only to be a first-time mother but also to have a DS baby, was the trouble of getting Max to nurse. He found it difficult to breastfeed as he just couldn't latch on. Apparently I didn't have the correct nipples! Max and I struggled for some time until I gathered the courage to ask for help. I explained my worries to the nurse on duty. Her response sent me reeling.

'Well, this is the kind of thing you get with these. They never feed well. Why don't you let someone else take care of him? There are places you know. Put him in a home, go on holiday, come back and have the baby you want. Your husband will leave you if you don't.'

She then turned and left the room. I was mortified. My instant reaction was to reach for the phone to call my mum. As usual she took my tears in her stride but this time she decided it was time to act. From the far-flung corners of Wiltshire she managed, uncharacteristically for her, to wreak havoc on the maternity unit of the hospital. Within the hour, only two nurses, sanctioned by my mother, were to be allowed access to my room. These nurses were genuinely kind and generous and helped me cope with my new baby. They were professional and treated me with respect and compassion rather than pity. From that moment on, no other nurses had any contact with me and for this I was hugely grateful. My mother had stepped in when I was too overwhelmed with the shock of a newborn baby to stand up for myself.

As well as the knowledge that my parents were backing us up, we also had Paul's mother Estelle on hand, as well as his father Gerry, who although living quite far away in South London, was always at the other end of the phone line. My sister Amanda also arrived regularly from Barnes. We welcomed her visits, not just for her company but also her delicious food that always made us feel better.

*

Now the news of Max's birth was out, flowers began to arrive in abundance. I'm sure the sentiments of the senders were honourable but to me the majority of deliveries smacked of sympathy, rather than congratulating me on the birth of my child. I know part of that was in my own head, but I only had that view because of the initial – mostly negative – reaction I'd had from the hospital. However, I couldn't escape the feeling that some of our 'well-wishers' thought it was most regrettable that we were not given the opportunity to have had Max aborted, and now he would be a drain on us and society. People still ask me today if I knew I was carrying a child with DS and I'm not sure how to answer. Are they implying that it would have been a blessing had I known? Would I then have been able to do everyone a massive favour and get rid of him? It's interesting to note that more young mothers rather than older ones have babies with DS, since older mothers generally have a screening for the condition.

In hindsight I'm pleased that I was in the dark. I would have surely been placed under tremendous pressure to have a termination. I would have been shocked and very scared and in that dreadful state I would have had to make a major decision. This irreversible path could have been taken by a 29-year-old woman, pregnant with her first child, with no idea what Down's syndrome entailed – and only the so-called experts with their own prejudices and agendas to guide her. Not the best of circumstances, I must say. I'm not against abortion; I strongly feel it is the given right of the mother to choose. We all have our own personal rules of moral conduct and it is not up to me to tell another person how to live their life. However, I know in my heart that to kill my child at any stage of its existence would haunt me for ever. I baulk at this new age of designer babies. I read of foetuses being terminated for cleft palate, club foot or minor abnormalities, and it fills me with horror. Who knows what impact such a decision would have had on my marriage? Perhaps Paul and I may have differed in our views and an entirely different set of circumstances could be facing us today?

The delivery of so many flowers also exposed people's difficulty in knowing how to react. Some seemed to be in total denial, refusing to see Max in any other light but as a bright new little human being, his presence posing no problem whatsoever to our future lives. It was understandable, but this denial was as difficult to stomach as the negativity. Perhaps I was being too harsh? After all, expecting people to empathise when even I didn't know how or what to feel wasn't fair. For a while afterwards I made an effort to see life from all points of view but now, following more than a decade of mixed messages and mistreatment – both intentional and unintentional from strangers and friends – I've toughened up. These days I am not so forgiving when a misguided comment is thrown my way. I have spent too long excusing and making allowances for entrenched attitudes. All it does is feed my anger. So now I let bad thoughts have their place. I admit to myself when I'm hurt from an ill-judged remark but I don't make excuses for it.

While I was obviously still emotionally and physically shaken, I began to think in more practical terms about the future with Max and where he might end up. From the start I knew there was no question of him not staying with me. I strongly believe that if an individual is institutionalised from any age their ability to thrive as an adult will be severely compromised. Any living soul in our society, who has sadly been touched by the wheels of bureaucracy and institutionalisation, is saddled with an additional burden. Love and security, the tools we are given in childhood for attaining a happy adult life that most of us take for granted, have never come their way. To receive no encouragement or support in one's early life can increase the chances of a person becoming broken or damaged. I felt if Max was with me and Paul, if we could provide a cherished, stable home full of love then he could thrive. Surely if I gave him the wholehearted gift of being his mother and did everything necessary, it would all work out all right?

It was only in 1971 that the Education Act deemed a person with Down's syndrome was actually entitled to an education. Until then, many people with DS were swept away into care homes, or hidden from society, deprived of what most of us take for granted. Since 1971 the avenues for educating people with DS have become clearer, but it is still by no means a straightforward process and there are still many preconceptions and prejudices that are yet to be overcome. But remarkably I have met adults with DS who against all odds have developed into charming, capable and responsible citizens. Despite the adversity they've faced they have managed to carve a full and satisfying life for themselves.

However, in the first few days after giving birth to Max I didn't have a clue about what Max, Paul and I were facing, and could only imagine enormous challenges ahead. Even so, I was determined that my son would not drop through the net. Sitting in that hospital room I came to a decision: I would give up my job.

I had always held the hope of returning to my work

in insolvency with the accounting firm, BDO Stoy Hayward. I enjoyed my work, and the friendships I had there. It gave me a chance to strut about in a suit feeling important. It taxed my brain, and it paid me well. But this world, full of deadlines and ambition, didn't make as much sense to me now. I don't want it to sound like some sort of epiphany or anything, but my values had changed, almost overnight. I could see no way of returning to my former life. I knew that I had only one shot at getting it right for Max, and I didn't feel I could do that properly if I was distracted by my job and Max was put in childcare for much of the day. At the time I thought I was taking the easy route; later on a friend would say I took the more difficult path.

Meanwhile Max had developed jaundice and was the colour of saffron. Whilst the nurses were not too alarmed, they kept a watchful eye on him. The stress of his jaundice and the difficulties I was having breast-feeding convinced me to transfer him entirely to bottled milk. This would enable me to monitor and increase his fluids. His condition meant that our stay in the hospital was prolonged, but I was so nervous about taking care of him on my own that I almost welcomed the delay in returning home. Other than the jaundice he was content to sleep and feed, giving me no bother. Still, I was unable to appreciate this delightfully good baby. I craved for him to wail with anger when he was returned to his perspex crib; I wanted him to grumble and complain if I was delayed with his feed. Instead he just slept quietly, unaware of the turmoil around him.

We soon had our first visit from the physiotherapist who made a detailed assessment of Max's talipes. One was much worse than the other, but if he was to avoid having an operation, or being placed in a cast, each foot would require heavy and regular physiotherapy. I was shown each exercise I was to perform on both of Max's feet every time his nappy was changed. This completely painless procedure would help to sustain regular mobility. The exercises took about five minutes, which sounds like nothing – and it was – but it became an unwanted chore. Once we returned home, we would have to bring Max back to hospital on a weekly basis to have his feet checked. Any progress he made would be closely monitored and a path of recovery planned.

My goal was to get his feet as straight as possible and hopefully avoid an operation. Max's jaundice was making him extra sleepy so we lay him in the sunlight as much as we could. My fear was that he had such a low IQ, he found it difficult to wake up at all. Having discovered that stimulation was vital, the coming years would see me stimulate my child to the point of absurdity. I learned and conquered every trick in the book, cramming my new-found expertise into his every waking minute, maximising interaction. Black-and-white mobiles over his cot, tin-foil shapes dangling by his changing mat, music, sensory touch toys: I had the lot. This continued for many years until my hysteria died down and common sense took over. I eventually began to realise that first and foremost I was his mother and that love, security and stability was what he needed most. Eventually Max would inform me what his requirements of me as a mother really were.

Our departure from hospital was eventually forced upon us by an emergency admission. Although it felt as if we were being unceremoniously evicted, Paul and I knew it was the best thing for us. I dread to think when we would have summoned enough courage to make the move on our own. With some trepidation we made our way back to our flat in Kilburn. Part of me was excited that we were starting our new life but I was also scared. I remember arriving home very clearly. Paul and I were sitting in the lounge staring vacantly at one another and Max was still in his portable car seat. Neither one of us had a clue what to do with this little chap, peacefully snoozing between us. Our immediate response to this dilemma was to purchase crates of champagne and begin a defiant, rampant celebration. Denial can be a life-preserving state of mind, and right now champagne was called for. We toasted our courage. We toasted our new family. We toasted Max, something we continued to do every day.

Shortly after returning home we were invited to have our genes screened. This seemed a responsible and sensible process to undertake. In hindsight it was possibly the wrong thing for us to do at the time and we could have done without it. We both gave vials of blood and cheek swabs to be analysed. On a positive note, it told us we were not carriers of any genetic abnormalities. The stone-faced scientist also told us that most people choose to terminate a pregnancy that has any sort of problem associated with it. Despite the good news that neither of us carried abnormal genes, we left his office feeling deflated. Society, it seemed to us, is pretty clear where it stands on welcoming a non-perfect baby.

On the whole Max looked like any other baby. It was painful to acknowledge that the almond shape of his eyes was a clear indication of the fact that he had DS but aside from that the only other obvious sign – really only visible to a professional – was the line on the palm of his hand. Look at your palm. The line an inch below your fingers splits off and branches out.

Max has one continuous line. It's one way of spotting DS in a baby. But otherwise, gazing at Max, sleeping sweetly in his basket, there was very little to give away his secret.

Chapter Three

30 September

*It's been raining hard today. Normally I'd adore it,
but today it's made me melancholy and down. But I
knew I just had to get outside in the open air to feel
free and not down-trodden, to smell autumn and to
see the rust and amber leaves before they disappear.*

*None of Max's therapists could make it today
so I forced myself to walk to Willesden to visit the
Toy Library. This isn't your average library; it's
specifically for babies and toddlers with Special
Needs. Max's therapist told me about it and I
should have gone ages ago, but I haven't as yet
mustered the courage. Luckily the rain stopped just
as Max and I left the house. He gets so excited
when we go out, he sees it as a big adventure. I told
myself all the way there to just 'run' with the visit.
Just breeze in and out, pick up a toy, it wouldn't be
a big deal. But as I approached the library, I began*

to sweat and feel nervous. I had agreed with myself
only to go in if I wanted to. I was confident I could
manage it. Well, I couldn't. I got there and just
couldn't go in. I immediately turned around and
trudged back home. I felt so very sad that I had not
been able to face it.

I was so fearful of seeing other babies with
Special Needs, particularly DS. I was terrified of
Max's future, and to be faced with another baby
with DS, perhaps a bit older than Max, clearly
demonstrating what was to come, was just something
I found unbearable. Fear and ignorance, that's what I
felt, the very traits I loathe in other people. I have
always faced my problems head on – but not today.
Today I experienced something new. Not only did I
not have the strength to face it: I didn't want to.

By the time Max was born, Paul and I had been
married for three years. When we had met I'd been
off men in a big way and had even considered giving
them up for good and buying a dog. It was New Year's
Eve and my good friend Wendy had insisted I accompany
her to the Everyman Restaurant in Hampstead. I
attended under sufferance. Having instigated the break-
up of a disastrous relationship I was pitifully broke,
contemplating a future of frightening mortgage payments

on my own. It was just another mistake in a long line of hideously unsuitable boyfriends: the pretty, the comedian, the rogue, the rebel. I knew I had the most appalling taste in men and had no desire to encourage another dead-end liaison of my own making. Wendy not only collected me from my attic flat in Kilburn, but paid for our meal and my journey home. She also led me to my husband and for that I shall be forever in her debt. After the midnight chimes and obligatory hysterical kissing, the restaurant turned into a party. Paul arrived at my side and asked me to dance. We've been dancing together ever since.

Paul is *so* not my type. Modest, kind, trustworthy, safe, and very clever, he is the antithesis of my previous boyfriends. The clever bit especially turned me on. I played hard to get for a while, but before too long, I came to realise that he was just what I had been waiting for. In addition to finding a best friend, I had fallen in love. That's not to say he doesn't drive me berserk on occasions (and I him!). He's a control freak and carries all the baggage that comes with that personality type. For many years getting him to open up and discuss things was like drawing blood from a stone. But he has such a capacity to love, learn and change. He is like a vintage wine: as he gets older he gets even better. I strongly believe meeting him was pure luck. It had nothing to do with any conscious selection criteria on my part!

Before Paul and I married, I never considered his merits as a father. I never paused to imagine him in a children's hospital ward, holding our child's hand as a nurse dug deep into Max's flesh, trying to find a vein and never succeeding first-time round. I never wondered if he'd cope with staying up all night cradling our son in his arms, wishing he could swap the pain for his own, as Max fought off yet another vicious viral infection. It never even occurred to me that any child of ours would suffer the sort of difficulties Max faced from the day he was born. It just felt right and I didn't hesitate. I didn't know how lucky I was until we had Max. In the coming years our marriage would be tested to the limit and time and time again we would come through. The strength of our marriage was tested even before we had Max as three months before conceiving him, Paul and I lost a baby. I was only in the first trimester of pregnancy, so technically speaking it was a miscarriage, but I still mourned the loss. I spent miserable hours in the Samaritan Hospital in Marylebone having a scan and internal examination, only to be told that our baby had no heartbeat. Paul waved goodbye to me as I was wheeled into theatre to have the dead baby removed. I know it happens all the time, but don't let anybody kid you that it is anything other than traumatic. I felt like part of me had been lost. Having a baby was something we had both longed for. If I shut my eyes for a split second I could exist in a world where the baby we were anticipating had arrived; the perfect reflection of all the best bits of me and Paul. However, even though Paul was hurting too, his love and support helped me to come through my miscarriage; like everything else, we got through this heartbreaking time together.

The first time I became pregnant, I tried to enrol in an antenatal class. I say 'tried' because they were all full up. How can that be? Do people actually apply the second the pregnancy test stick turns blue? Or, God forbid, prior to conception? Are their first thoughts 'Wow I'm pregnant! I must apply for my place at the local antenatal class'? Perhaps they're just more organised than I am! The second time around I was much more savvy and got my application in quickly.

In hindsight, I question why I was so desperate to join a group. Normally I had avoided groups for as long as I can remember. Perhaps I thought that joining it would bring me one step closer to being a mother and give me some sort of security? By the time the classes started all the women had big round tummies and the discussion focused on birthing pools, breastfeeding and epidurals. The meetings were held at the house of the lady who ran them, Eileen. Even though Paul took the mickey a bit, we obediently went every week.

Very soon after we took Max home we started to receive news that baby after healthy baby had arrived. Nervous and unsure of the reaction of others, Paul and I found it hard to contemplate hooking up with other parents from the class. We both felt it was easier and less traumatic to let go of that part of our lives. There was, however, one couple from the group whom we did feel comfortable with. Rachel and Sam. Ten days after I'd had Max, Rachel gave birth to her daughter Daisy. From then on we formed a connection and started to spend afternoons with one another, chatting over cups of tea and playing with our babies. I thought she was lovely and she seemed to have great empathy with me and my situation. Rachel was a special needs teacher at a primary school. She knew what children with DS faced and I felt comforted by her enthusiastic and passionate attitude to all children and their individual requirements.

Despite Rachel's acceptance of Max and her attitude towards him, it hurt me to watch Daisy climb the stairs to our flat wearing her first pair of shoes, when my own son still couldn't sit up. It took enormous willpower on my part to fight off emotions of bitterness and jealousy. Rachel's daughter was cruising through her first few months of life, crashing through each milestone with ease and minimum effort, something my son would never do. But Rachel seemed understanding and generous about it all. I grew more and more fond of her and enjoyed visiting her house in Hampstead Garden Suburb. It was a tiny three-bedroom semi, surrounded by a forest of shrubs and trees.

It was about this time that I joined the post-natal group of my antenatal parenting classes. Why I did not hesitate to join, when my experience of the antenatal classes left little to be desired, still leaves me bemused. I am entirely content and happy with my own company and while I hugely value my friends I can count them on the fingers of one hand. I don't do acquaintances: either you're my mate and we have a truth between us or you're not.

Therefore it may have been a touch of masochism, or perhaps it was an iron determination to enjoy all the available experiences motherhood brings that brought me to that place. It took all my nerve to drag myself and Max to the first meeting. If you met me, you would never imagine I was shy. I have robust opinions on most things, love to make people laugh and can actually get a bit too forthright on occasions. But essentially I am shy, and meeting anyone for the first time is as daunting a task for me now as it was that day.

Some eight mothers and their tiny babies were crammed into one volunteer mother's flat. I felt over-whelmed at once. It was far too many people for my liking and I had to work hard to quell my feelings of claustrophobia and panic. There was lots of noise as these new mothers eagerly shared their birthing stories. To me they seemed so smugly self-satisfied at the little bundles of pure genius they had so miraculously produced, all of them boasting and preening over their babies. I wanted to slap them. They clutched their red child-health record books that documented each little stage in their child's development, lovingly plotted on a nice, reassuring graph. With this they were able to justify, examine and compare.

I didn't have this red record book. My GP had already warned me that Max's growth and weight could not be monitored on a 'normal' graph. Surrounded by these young mothers, detailing how much weight their child had gained that week or when they could expect their baby to roll over, I had little option but to keep my head down and remain quiet.

It was almost incomprehensible to me. Here I was, with Max, fiercely proud of him, celebrating each tiny milestone with gusto, desperately worried that an everyday, run-of-the-mill cold or infection could evolve into something life threatening, while all these mothers seemed to be concerned about was their babies meeting developmental deadlines set down in some book. All I saw was perfectly healthy, adorable babies. But all they seemed to see was different ways of introducing new worries, anxieties and neuroses into what I saw as their perfectly normal, lovely, well-to-do lives.

Maybe I was being too harsh on these mothers, and I admit I was envious of their healthy babies. But I didn't wish any bad karma upon them. The truth is that I was drowning in their company. I couldn't relate to them and what they were going through; my issues just seemed too different to theirs to have any sort of connection. To be honest, I don't think it was quite my scene anyway, regardless of what was happening with Max. If he had been born 'normal' I still think they would have driven me insane.

Finding the meetings a strain, but still persisting in attending, I dragged my mum with me on one occasion. Later as we shared a quiet cup of tea she suggested I contact Evelyn, one of the other mothers there. It seems Mum had spotted a discontentment bubbling under Evelyn's demeanour. It took a few days and some gentle nagging on Mum's part, but I finally plucked up the courage and called. I lost no time with pleasantries and explained how I felt about the ghastly post-natal group. 'Oh my God, I'm so glad you rang me, I feel exactly the same,' was her welcome reply.

Evelyn was not one to gush over her son, Joseph. While she patently adored him, she managed to do so without acting as if he was sent to save the world. We plotted to form our own sub-group. It would be just the two of us, without the yummy mummies of North London. The group tried to persuade us we needed to stay, but we left them to it and set about enjoying our new babies in a more tolerable, gentle way.

Chapter Four

3 August

The past few weeks have been truly terrible and I'm wondering if I have the post-natal blues. The knowledge that Max has DS is so final: there is no cure, no remission, and no wrong diagnosis. And what's more the buck stops with me – and Paul – but definitely, definitely me. To be trapped by one's own child is terrifying. I love him more than life itself but I want a life too. As naive parents-to-be, one of the aspects of parenthood that frightened us both was the thought when any future children left our loving nest there was no guarantee that they'd keep up regular contact. It seems we now have the reverse; Max will never *have the opportunity to leave us. Good or bad, it's a fact.*

What most frightens me is that the harsh reality of his true handicap will unfold slowly and cruelly over time. I sometimes forget the degree of his

*special needs and I kid myself that he's just a bit
behind. I weakly fall into the common trap for
parents in my position, the line that 'my child is
different: he's a wonder child, supremely gifted,
blessed and more special than the rest'. Is that true
or am I just deceiving myself? His future terrifies
me. It's like a tsunami, slowly but surely gaining
momentum and no matter how fast we run it will
catch up with us. As I kiss and cuddle him, all I see
is a glorious, adorable, lovely baby. But in time he
will have the mind of a baby and the body of a
thirty-five-year-old. What am I to do then?*

The summer heat brought with it an appointment
back to St Mary's Hospital in Paddington to see a
paediatric cardiologist. Paul was away on business: his
job as Director of Advertising and Marketing with
Warner Brothers took him to LA three or four times a
year, as well as to other less glitzy destinations. As most
people who fly for work know, it's not as glamorous as it
sounds and it was something Paul and I both found difficult. Now, at a time when I desperately needed support, I
felt even more alone. Still there was very little option but
to get on with it and that's exactly what we did.

Although I was lonely, I found it easy to look after
Max as he was a remarkably good and contented baby.

Sometimes I think that if I'd only had him as a second child, I would have known to treasure him all the more. I would have appreciated his docile ways and love of sleeping, instead of fretting about the level of his IQ and the excessive stimulation he required. I could have put the kettle on, sat back and enjoyed him.

On the day of the appointment I arrived at the hospital and entered the children's outpatients department only to be confronted by a swarm of people. Surely we weren't all here to see the same doctor? Oh yes we were: the entire length of the corridor and all the little pockets that led off it were crammed full of nervous, fretful parents with tiny young babies, waiting to see one cardiologist. I shuffled myself and Max over to one side so I could lean against a wall, but eventually ended up sitting on the floor. If I'd been the person I am today, I would have politely demanded answers as to why we were all in this mess. But I wasn't: I was just a new mother with a fragile baby and so, like many of the parents who were waiting with me, I had no strength left for any sort of confrontation. I just waited, fretting. I waited and waited, for *five* hours, and with each passing minute I kept imagining the worst for Max. But I was too scared to walk away, too weak to complain.

Thankfully, I plan my life pre-empting eventualities. I always arrive a little early for any engagement just so

I have that extra time in hand. My handbag is full of pain killers, tampons, plasters. So thankfully I was well prepared with food and nappies for Max and our long wait that day. Our turn finally arrived and we were welcomed into a small, stiflingly hot room, where our cardiologist sat. He looked frustrated, exhausted and slightly cross, but immediately apologised for our abominable waiting time, and I was impressed with how he calmly placed all such irritations to one side and gave me and Max his full attention. He was one of the first professionals to greet me humanely, with respect, honesty and empathy.

After a thorough examination of Max and his miniature heart he said that although Max had a large hole in his heart, it would be prudent to allow his body the opportunity to heal itself. There would be two opportunities for the hole to close: the first would be his infant years, up to the age of approximately seven, and then again when Max hit puberty. He said he could close the hole immediately, if that's what we wanted, but was careful to point out the perils of such heart surgery.

These would include Max being placed on a bypass machine while the procedure was carried out. This would involve his heart being stopped and a machine taking over. Once the surgery was completed, his heart would then have to be restarted. This came with its own harrowing complications and could result in it not starting again. If it did start, Max could be left with kidney or liver failure, as well as a long list of other terrifying complications. If the operation succeeded, Max would still be left with probably his biggest threat: post-operative infection. Max's poor immune system meant that any infection would pose a serious risk to his life. Even the anaesthetic could be perilous.

In the cardiologist's opinion, Max would benefit from the healing properties of time. We were welcome to seek advice from elsewhere, and he reiterated that if we couldn't bear the thought of waiting to see what would happen, then he would close the hole. Max was not presenting any physical signs that the hole was causing him distress. In the future an operation could by no means be ruled out, in fact it was almost inevitable, but waiting to see whether the heart would heal itself was a safer option.

It made sense to me. Even over a decade ago, the spectre of MRSA was beginning to thread its way amongst the sick and weak in every hospital up and down the country. If Max caught MRSA, he didn't stand a chance.

The cardiologist assured me that a close eye was to be kept on Max, and he ran through signs I should watch for, mainly Max becoming breathless and turning blue. He wanted to see Max every four months for echoes and cardiograms. The doctor once again apologised for the long wait, and I then asked if we could see him privately. Whilst the care would be identical, he did admit that the waiting conditions would be more pleasant. When I gave birth to Max, I was covered under the medical insurance provided by Paul's employers, so he was covered from birth automatically, regardless of what conditions he had. I had no need to think twice, we were going private.

Although what I had just heard wasn't really unexpected, once we were in the safety of the car the river of tears came. I suddenly felt very scared and miserable; I felt powerless to protect my child. I would have swapped my life for his in an instant, made a pact with the devil and paid any ransom to repair my beloved son. I asked myself what on earth I had done to produce a child with such a disadvantage?

Perhaps it was the Roaccutane I took as a teenager? From early adolescence I'd suffered the distressing condition of acute acne and was covered in angry red, pus-oozing spots. They weren't just all over my face, but they also appeared on the tops of my arms and thighs, shoulders and chest. I was miserable and the pimples made me feel horribly self-conscious. I always think it's a nasty trick that just at the point of puberty, teenagers have the added burden of spots to deal with; the stuff going on in your head is difficult enough. I was one of the unluckiest ones and each day would have to cope with people staring at me in the corridors at school and in the street. They would stop and look back at me and I wanted to disappear. I tried everything within my power to prevent these hideous outbreaks but nothing worked. Along with all the skin treatments commercially available and meticulous hygiene, I went on the pill for a bit and took a low-grade antibiotic too, but nothing came close to getting rid of it.

In desperation, my parents sent me to a skin specialist, who, as well as making up his own solutions of antibiotic to be applied directly to the skin, recommended that I take a drug called Roaccutane. He promised it would eradicate the acne and leave my skin blemish free. At the same time he made no secret of the disturbing side effects that would accompany this 'miracle' cure. Roaccutane works by eradicating excretion from the sebaceous glands deep within the skin, well before a spot has had a chance to form. It is also extremely toxic, which meant that if I were to fall pregnant the developing foetus would almost certainly be deformed. I therefore needed to be clear in my mind that I would be happy to terminate any such pregnancy. I seem to recall he even made me sign a form accepting that I had been fully informed of such perils. I was only fifteen and not sexually active so had no hesitation in accepting the deal: I just wanted to get rid of my disgusting spots. Once I started the treatment, the speed with which they disappeared was nothing short of sensational. I was jubilant.

My parents had massive misgivings about such an invasive drug and coaxed me into considering returning the Roaccutane and surviving on the antibiotic alone. They were not comfortable with the idea of such a powerful drug polluting their young daughter's system. They pointed out that beauty is only skin deep and fades with time, and how it was inevitable that there would always be someone in the room more beautiful than you. They spoke of how beauty radiates from within, a beauty stronger than any superficial exterior. I knew they were right in theory and I liked their big picture of life, but like many young women I could never believe that I was truly attractive.

The hideousness of the spots made it very hard to go back to the skin specialist and surrender the Roaccutane. Eventually I did. I now think it is more than a little ironic that my own son has a label plastered across his face that separates him from others, and leaves him open to judgement, not just aesthetically, but in all aspects of his being.

The thing that was nagging me was this: was I, for

the sake of my own vanity, responsible for giving my own son Down's syndrome? As it so often did, the sadness and guilt soon translated into a chilling fear. Would I have to bury him? Would I have to pick out a tiny white coffin that would steal him away from me for ever? Would I have to say goodbye so soon after he had arrived?

That day, after the appointment with the cardiologist and still sitting in my parked car, all these thoughts of despair going through my head, I felt alone and very, very low. I picked up Max from his car seat and cradled him in my arms. He was like a little rag doll. Standard babies have muscle tone that renders them strong and tense; you can feel it when you pick them up. They're fragile, but you can detect a slight rigidity to their muscles. Babies with DS, like Max, have no such strength; if you fail to fully support their body it will hang limp and frail.

I breathed in his intoxicating smell – the very same smell that all new babies have – and made a wish, silently promising that if it were granted I would never ask for anything again: please, please let Max live so I can watch him grow and enjoy his precious life.

Max was only three months old and I'd already fed hundreds of pounds into hospital car-parking machines. We were spending a lot of time there, for Max's talipes as well as his heart. He had removable casts on both feet that he was required to wear all day every day, except when I removed them so he could have a bath or if I was performing the endless exercise and massage routines. It was looking increasingly likely that he may need an operation on one of his feet, a thought I dreaded. Max would be forced to go through a lot of pain before, during and after. But obviously I was not going to compromise his ability to walk, and therefore if an operation was necessary he would have it.

However, I was determined to make every possible effort to avoid an operation: if I was diligent about his exercises and wearing of the casts, we might just make it. Poor Max: it was a very hot summer and the casts were sweaty and heavy. They didn't look that great either. Since I couldn't put him in cute little babygros, he ended up wearing little vests with cardigans, which in hindsight was absolutely fine, but once more I felt cheated of the joy of putting my baby into the clothes I wanted him to wear. Nothing about this was what I had expected when I was pregnant, nothing. When Max was in my womb I would dream of all the adorable outfits I would be able to parade him in. Okay, it sounds small and petty but it mattered to me, especially because it seemed that other mothers enjoyed such privileges without question.

Back from the hospital I had the difficult task of

conveying all the information I'd gathered from the cardiologist to Paul, who was on the other side of the world. The science of the situation was both complicated and frightening and we found it hard to absorb it all.

At times it felt as if Paul and I were living a dual life. In striking contrast to our insular world where we were doing our best to look after Max's health and keep him – and us – safe from prejudice, Paul's job required him to mix with the beautiful people in the film business. He may not have seen himself as one of them, but it was his business to operate in that largely superficial world.

Not long after his return from LA, Paul had to oversee yet another movie premiere. I always did my best to accompany him to such functions, mainly because he liked to have me around, but also because it was a chance to dress up and go out. I liked my occasional glimpses of this world and the buzz that went with it and even though it was full of 'luvvies' and divas, London was far more down to earth than LA. But with Max in our family, my perspective had changed. I found the attitude of the so-called stars and the sheer amount of excess hard to take. The truth is that I had never really been at home in that life, but now I had a get-out clause.

Chapter Five

19 November

Like some heavenly sign, or a declaration of a divine promise, something enchanting and wonderful happened today. Max grinned at me. A beaming smile from cheek to chubby cheek, and a sparkle deep from within his adorable twinkling eyes. Since that smile the sun has shone and I feel like I have spent the day cocooned in a colourful blanket with nothing to touch me.

I remember the morning I woke up paralysed. Not literally, but mentally and emotionally. The thought of showering or getting dressed suddenly seemed a thought too far. I'd had eight months of life with Max and while I was busy figuring out how to care for my son, the black dog of depression had crept up and dug a hole in my brain. I tried to carry on my daily routine as best I could. While I had neither the strength nor the inclination to properly attend to my own needs, I was still there for Max, albeit on autopilot. After a week of seeing his wife become a mute shadow of herself, Paul became concerned and insisted I go to my GP who immediately sent me to the Charter Nightingale Hospital in Lisson Grove.

I sat in a room with Max cuddled on my lap while a man, whose task it was to do the initial patient assessment, asked me questions. He wanted to know how I was feeling and how I thought the depression had manifested itself, but one question stood out: had I ever contemplated suicide? I paused considerably before replying, which I think he saw as an attempt to dodge the truth. It wasn't. I was simply searching for the right words to explain myself. I told him that suicide was not an option for me (of course, I'm not suggesting it is a tolerable option for anyone) and that my son would keep me on this earth because just the fact of his existence automatically justified mine.

I returned home that evening to receive a call from a Dr Elsa Epen. She wanted to see me the next day. I had never experienced any type of therapy before and therefore had no preconceived ideas or prejudices. My initial problem was that I was barely functioning so it took a huge effort just to turn up. I remember sitting in the waiting room alarmed by the outrageously thin, sick-looking young girls and intrigued by the odd respectable-looking businessman. Madness looked disturbingly normal.

For me, therapy soon became akin to being in a secluded garden. It was a private, safe place where I could say anything and be anyone, however ugly. It took time; I felt dreadfully uncomfortable answering questions put to me by a perfect stranger whom I knew nothing about, save for her professional credentials.

Ten years on I know no more about the personal life of Dr Epen than I did then. It's a very odd, one-sided relationship. There's no batting questions and ideas back and forth, no sense of dialogue as we understand it in the outside world. Dr Epen immediately suggested I went on medication. She explained that my stress and anxiety had embedded itself into me so that my brain was failing to produce any serotonin – the naturally occurring chemical that helps you feel good. I was going to have to give it a helping hand.

Without even considering the options, I flatly refused. I was terrified of any mind-altering drugs and had never been tempted into the world of recreational drug use, not because of any moral 'holier than thou' attitude, but because I was just scared of anything I was unable to control. I'll admit that I had been influenced by articles in the press that suggested that people who started taking Prozac committed suicide within days. I now know that much of this is sensational and there is a lot more to the truth behind those headlines. Dr Epen did not attempt to coerce me in any way and that increased my respect for her. Nonetheless it would take another eight years – during which the black dog would run rampant, terrorising and immobilising me – before I relented and reached out for medication.

Meanwhile Dr Epen suggested that exercise and abstinence from alcohol would help my recovery. Visit after visit, she gently reminded me that I needed to help myself. I agreed, but the problem was that I loved drinking; it gave me a much-needed escape from my problems and quelled the persistent anxiety that gnawed at me. Just a glass or two every evening helped to offset worries about what I might be dealing with next. A fever erupting out of control, a bacterial infection that could lead to deadly septicaemia or Max's heart showing signs of failure were always possible dangers. I never sank into pure oblivion; half a bottle of red wine or champagne would do the trick. There were no binges or drunken tirades, just a steady regular fix. Despite the doctor's recommendations I wasn't going to give up alcohol or even pretend to.

To Dr Epen's credit she understood and never played hardball, having worked out that if she chose that particular route I would close up and probably end up lying to her. I did follow her advice about exercise which I did every day for at least half an hour. We already had an exercise bike that I hated. It was boring but I dutifully pedalled for twenty minutes every day. I tried incorporating reading, watching television, and music into these sessions but it didn't make them any more palatable. Even so, I surprised myself with my grit and determination. Not only did I stick to the bike, I then dragged myself off to the local swimming pool. There I would trudge up and down the lanes, trying not to think of what substances – noxious or otherwise – were in the pool. Max would be in his little portable car seat, peacefully sleeping at one end of the pool where I could keep an eye on him.

At her request, Paul made a visit to Dr Epen to be given a brief introduction to depression and how it was affecting me. The idea was that he would have a better understanding of the condition, so he could help me. He also realised that although I was not myself, I was still sane and that our child was in safe hands. My sessions with Dr Epen continued every week and she was amazed and pleased at my continued strength and determination, as was I. During our time together we discovered I had a predisposition to bleak thoughts. Since the age of 13, I can recall gloomy, dark periods

Sandy Lewis

looming over my adolescence. I suspect my saving grace was my major participation in sports. I ran for the school in cross-country and 1,500 metres and was captain of the hockey team. Sport was positively encouraged and applauded at my school and made for a natural, unquestionable path of inclusion. It now seems that it unwittingly saved me from experiencing depression a lot earlier. The arrival of Max had been like a trip switch setting off stress, then anxiety and finally depression.

I told no one what was happening. Even 10 years ago, depression was still a bit of a dirty secret. If I'd broken a leg or was suffering from diabetes, then my news would have been safe and manageable. A physical illness would have been received with open, caring arms, sympathy and offers of advice and help. My feeling was that, if I put my depression out there, the reaction from people I knew may have been severely judgemental. One of the problems with depression is that the word itself is a blanket description of a condition that has many different forms. There are many people who are mildly depressed from time to time who will most likely move on without intervention. At the other end of the scale there are people whose chemistry predisposes them to serious clinical depression and who are literally immobilised without medication. In between there are people like me who may have a predisposition waiting to be triggered by some life event. While I was fully capable of functioning (albeit in a mechanical way) my misery was transferring itself from my mind to my body and on top of the despair I was feeling, I was utterly physically exhausted.

When life dishes out adversity, it does so in job lots. One day during this period Max had been struggling to keep down fluids. In the middle of the night he developed a fever. With our anxiety levels off the scale, we called a doctor and a locum arrived within the hour. While I remember neither his name nor his face, I can vividly recall his words.

'What happened here? How come he's Down's then? Did you not have a test? This won't do will it? You're so young too. I guess you must have slipped through the net. What a shame.'

We were shocked but didn't say a word. Part of me just wanted him to do his job and get out of my flat as quickly as possible. Neither of us had the strength nor the desire to defend the existence of our son. Paul raced off to an all-night chemist for the necessary antibiotics to fix our baby, but the pain caused by the doctor's words – and I am sure they were not intentionally cruel – could not be fixed so easily. They hit us at a time when we were feeling very exposed and vulnerable. The trauma of Max's birth was still having a profound effect upon us. Although we were trying to look after Max together, we were each fighting our own individual demons. In addition there was the shock to the system that all new parents go through: the lack of sleep, the need to establish routines and the necessity to incorporate a new, small person, entirely dependent on us, into our existing lives. And then there is that covert pressure, one that I am sure many new parents feel: the feeling that you're supposed to look like you're coping and enjoying it all but you're not, not all of it anyway.

In an attempt to catch a ray of carefree family life we decided that we would brave our first holiday and booked a two-week break in Sardinia. Max was so small I was able to make a bed for him out of the pull-down food tray on the plane. On the other hand, I had put on so much weight I was heavier than when I was pregnant. Clearly despair had done something to my brain because my fashion sense had deserted me, leading me to pack a lime green, shiny, lycra swimming costume in my suitcase. With my lily-white arms and legs protruding, it was the most unflattering garment I could have chosen to wear. On our return home, I pinned a photograph of me in the hideous swimsuit to the fridge door. It was an excellent reminder of how I had let myself go. I had been eating indiscriminately, always dipping biscuits in mugs of tea, and relying on take-aways to give me short-term comfort. Food may have helped take the edge off the demands of first-time motherhood, but it did little for my figure or self esteem.

We stumbled through our holiday with relatively few hiccups. Max gave us a passing scare when he developed an alarming heat rash, but we soon realised this was just peculiar to his own metabolism and that he was fine. We returned home with new strength and vigour and made the major decision to move house. After all, Max was soon going to have to attend school and we wanted to be near the very best we could find.

Rachel had been very useful in helping us make a decision about Max's education. From information available to us, we understood that the general consensus was that children with DS should attend mainstream schools and this appealed to us. Rachel told us about a school with a tremendous reputation in North London called Brooklands. The catchment area was incredibly tight; you literally had to be in one of a handful of streets to be certain of a guaranteed place. In terms of finding a house, there wasn't much room to manoeuvre. We found and bought a small three-bedroom semi that happened to be in the same cul-de-sac as Rachel's. The house was dinky but very pretty and had a gigantic garden. We had to stretch ourselves financially, but we were determined to seek out the very best for our son.

Just before we moved, I went for a drink with my friend Emma. We made a night of it, tucking ourselves in at the local wine bar, nibbling on tapas and consuming large quantities of red wine. Towards the end of the evening, when I confess we were both rather tipsy, the subject turned to producing a healthy baby and that's when everything went pear-shaped. Emma was very clear that she wouldn't hesitate in terminating a handicapped foetus. Having poked the boundaries of discretion and sensitivity, she then brought the walls tumbling down.

'And anyway,' she said, 'even though I have a second cousin with Down's syndrome, we've not got any poisoned blood running on our side of the family, so there's no way I would produce a child with such a poor gene pool. I've no need to worry.'

Did I really hear her say that? Coming from an individual who knew my situation only too well, the remark was both insensitive and passively savage. I'm fascinated to know what goes on inside people's heads after they've delivered comments like this. Are they angry with themselves? Do they feel regret and embarrassment? Perhaps her own deep fear of having a disabled child allowed her demons to take over and say things she wouldn't ordinarily? I was flabbergasted and couldn't wait to leave; it was all I could do to pay my tab, say goodbye and bolt home. I had no strength to challenge Emma: she had wounded me and my thoughts were sad and tearful, and only later would they turn to anger and sharp, quick-witted replies. The fact remains that Paul and I have had many hurtful things said to us over the years but no one has ever apologised. Apparently Emma never even remembered what she'd said, but I did. Since then I've had no desire to speak to her.

On a more positive note, Max was getting encouraging feedback from the hospital regarding his talipes. The exercises had achieved all that could be desired and both his feet were soft and supple. The physiotherapist said we could now leave the casts off and just concentrate on the exercises and massaging. It looked like we might avoid an operation and both Paul and I were ecstatic. Just the thought of not spending so much time at the hospital would be a luxury. I felt blessed.

Chapter Six

14 May

Max and I went to Brent Cross shopping centre today. It was mid-morning and packed, with not a parking space in sight. I managed to spot a free space in a disabled bay so I parked with Max's blue badge clearly visible when this vile woman pulled up alongside me. Her face leered at me as she shouted, 'This is a disabled bay, you know.'

'Yes, I am aware of that, I do have a blue badge.'

'Yeah right.'

Now I'm all for policing the abuse of designated parking, but I do wish people would wait before shooting their mouths off. In a rage I marched up to her window. She didn't even have a disabled badge; she was just having a go because she was miffed that there was no parking.

'Don't "yeah right" me. My son has Down's syndrome and is fully entitled to a badge. Listen, if

you feel left out, I'd gladly swap. Your kid can have the Down's syndrome, with the blue badge thrown in for free. I assure you, it's far from a perk.'

Give her credit: she did look suitably guilty after checking out Max's giveaway face, as he lay in my arms. How dare she assume I had in some way violated the system and was languishing with glee in the only free parking space? While I had managed to produce a snappy reply, if the truth be told the woman won in the end. Try as I might to push the incident from my mind, I failed and it totally ruined my morning. Why can't people just fuck off and leave me alone?

At the age of two Max started at a local nursery in Hendon which welcomed children with special needs as well as those without. We hoped this mixed environment would help Max to develop on every level, in particular his very limited communication skills. At this stage he had no discernible speech and was still unable to walk, but he could finally sit up unaided and drink from a spouted cup. He already had a pre-school teacher called Hilary, who had been visiting us at home for the last year and it was her suggestion that he attend the nursery. While I was hesitant, I couldn't afford to disregard any positive input

Max might receive. Paul and I went to visit the nursery, which was tucked away behind the back of a church. It was not glossy in any way or spilling over with brand-new toys. In fact, it was surprisingly tatty but it did have a wonderful atmosphere. A group of caring ladies, headed by a priceless individual called Dawn, had created an environment that I felt would be of great benefit to Max.

Nonetheless I was rather apprehensive. Not only was Max still a very long way behind his peers, but it was also difficult to know when he would reach certain milestones. For example, he could sit up for relatively long periods of time, but was fragile and could easily topple backwards. And here I was contemplating handing over this little baby, with very few marked delays in his development and lots of idiosyncrasies, to a place teeming with sturdy little children, bumping into each other and charging about. I worried about him being away from people he knew but I realised it made sense. He wouldn't be entirely on his own; he was to have a carer who would be totally responsible for him. So although I was reluctant, we turned up on our first Monday morning ready for fun. I needn't have worried.

He fell into the arms of Helen, his newly elected carer, who frankly could not have been a better choice if I had combed the streets of London for an eternity.

She was devoted to his every need and when I returned after his two-hour session, I could see that she and Max had formed an immediate bond. It was still very hard. I was shy and so was Helen, so we took a long time to get to know one another. At the beginning I would return home from dropping off Max and fret for two hours, repeatedly checking the clock for when I could return to collect him. I always arrived ridiculously early.

Helen is a focused, calm person who has a down-to-earth, pragmatic and gentle approach to life. She has a daughter called Gemma who is only a couple of years older than Max. A beautiful child with golden hair cascading down her back, Gemma would often be at the nursery with her mother for one reason or another and Max simply adored her. It turned out that Helen was a single parent. Her husband abandoned her when her daughter was a very young baby. Helen woke up one morning and he had gone. There were rumours via his bemused mother that he had gone to Spain. Not only did he leave without any warning or explanation, but he failed to provide any financial support to his wife and child. Helen gathered all her strength and devoted herself to her daughter, coping on a very slender income. I have nothing but the utmost respect for her, not only as a mother, but as a survivor and a friend.

Eventually I stopped fretting and began to look

forward to my two hours of freedom each morning. The time passed so quickly, I barely had a chance to complete the numerous tasks I had set myself, before returning to pick up Max. Despite his inability to talk, his lively, cheeky personality soon had all the ladies at the nursery wrapped around his little finger. Thinking about it now, I am reminded of what a peaceful time it was; the calm before the storm. As I've said earlier, I wish I could have enjoyed these moments more but that is just human nature. If only we didn't have to wait until after the event to acquire wisdom.

As well as learning to cope with Max I was adapting to life without work. I believe I underestimated the effect that particular shift was having on me. There was the value I had attributed to earning my own money and, perhaps even more importantly, the feeling that I had my own definite place in society. Don't get me wrong; I wasn't unhappy with my choice but I missed work. I missed the fun, the friendships, the flirting and the power. Occasionally I would still return to BDO Stoy Hayward to visit my former workmates. They welcomed me enthusiastically but it was not the same. I had moved on and so had they. We no longer had the glue of those day-to-day experiences to hold us together.

Yet while some friendships evaporated, new ones were created. A warm, friendly couple and their two adorable sons came into our lives. Con and Ti and their boys, Joshua and Luke, originated from Liverpool and while they now lived in Sevenoaks, they held firm to their northern virtues of hospitality, generosity and charm. Con was a work colleague of Paul's and they had struck up an easy and strong friendship. Soon we were receiving invitations to stay the weekend with them. Paul is marginally more outgoing than me and thought it was a great idea, so off we went. They welcomed us with open arms and made us feel that Max was just as amazing and accomplished as either one of their sons. That was over 13 years ago and we have become very close since. Ti is now one of my dearest friends, a very clever woman with a huge capacity to love. My world is a brighter, happier place for having her as a treasured friend.

Another woman who would also become a close friend was Rebecca: feisty, loquacious, funny and full of attitude. We actually met at a monthly meeting of Parents of Down's syndrome (PODS). These gatherings were useful opportunities to swap information and support one another. Rebecca arrived with her new son Robbie and was the first person I'd got close to who had a child with DS. Robbie was two years younger than Max but I felt Rebecca knew far more than me already. While this was mildly unnerving, it was also a comfort.

Her relentless optimism also helped to calm me during periods of uncertainty. Rebecca formed friendships with other mothers whose children were much younger than Max, and encouraged me to do the same, but I was unable to conquer my shyness and so never fully immersed myself in their circle. From time to time, I would attend meetings or events where I would bump into them, but in my head I always felt like an outsider. Later, time and circumstances would allow me to grow closer to all these women and see at first hand their determination and strength in achieving the very best for their children.

For a few months after Max started nursery, we trundled along quite happily. But one day, during a routine nappy change, I noticed Max was bleeding from his penis. His nappy was stained with blood and his penis looked sore and inflamed. My immediate response was to hit the hysteria button, my reaction to everything in those early days. We managed to reach the GP's surgery in double-quick time and were seen by our doctor, who immediately reassured us by saying that Max had a urinary tract infection, which was perfectly treatable. However, in order to prescribe the right medications she would need a sample of Max's urine. This proved to be enormously tricky, since babies do not pee on demand. Following the normal procedure in a situation like this, a bag was fitted around Max's groin in the hope that some urine would be collected. Finally after hours of frustration we managed to obtain a small sample.

As well as treating the infection with antibiotics, the doctor advised us that a scan of Max's bladder and urinary tract would be beneficial. Many cases of kidney disease in later life can be attributed to a neglected urinary infection in childhood. It would be a good idea to be sure the infection had been totally eradicated and give Max a thorough check-up at the same time.

We saw an excellent paediatrician, who not only confirmed that Max was in fine working order but recommended a particular antibiotic called zithromax. Although expensive this antibiotic only needed to be administered once a day. This was fantastic news, since the standard antibiotic prescribed in such circumstances must be administered three times a day, and this was a massive challenge as Max was not cooperative when it came to taking medicine and strongly fought any attempts to treat him. From then on, whenever Max was ill – which was quite often – our GP showed true kindness by overlooking the huge cost of this drug and prescribing it. Small acts of kindness like this went a very long way in taking the sting out of our over-stressed lives. Sometimes it's the smallest gestures that are most effective and most appreciated.

Our annual holiday was upon us and we were determined to join the rest of the world in enjoying our time
in the sun. We had planned a trip to Tuscany, staying in
a small villa with a pool all to ourselves. I can honestly
say it was the most miserable holiday Paul and I ever
had. The place was beautiful (even if the electricity
continually tripped out for most of the day), rustic and
lush. Remote and isolated from the beaten track, it
meant we could be undisturbed until we chose to
venture out. But, as the saying goes, you take yourself
with you, and Paul and I were still trapped by grief,
despair and shock. We were still adjusting to this world
we'd been catapulted into. As soon as we squared off
one anxiety, another would surface. We were miserable
and began to bicker and squabble with each other. It
was a low point in our marriage but it was also a major
turning point.

That holiday marked the moment we both woke up
to reality. Reluctantly we were both forced to acknowledge that our situation was not transitional, but was for
real. Our lives and our marriage could go one of two
ways. Perhaps the mere fact that we both had this overwhelming love for Max propelled us to find a way to
face the future together. It was not some epiphany but a
slow drip of acceptance and maturity. It would have been
easy to turn our sadness and sorrow into ammunition

against one another but we managed to find composure and unity. And, yes, perhaps luck played a part too. We will never understand what divine intervention determines our future but we returned from that holiday in Tuscany with the option, however bleak, to go our separate ways. It was never voiced, but it was definitely there, hanging in the air. But from then on we grew even more united and, yes, we grew up.

Chapter Seven

12 June

Max was terribly unwell on Monday. He'd been ill all weekend and I got to the stage where I needed him checked by a doctor or I was going to go mad. Thank goodness the reception staff and doctors at Temple Fortune Health Centre are so nice to us.

We saw Dr Karen Grossmark, our usual doctor, who's lovely. She had a good look at Max and calmly suggested I go home, pack a bag and get him over to the Royal Free Hospital as soon as possible. She'd warn them we were on our way and advised me to pack some things for myself as well as for Max in case I needed to spend the night at the hospital with him. The sense of urgency made me speechless with worry.

Within the space of half an hour, I had gone home, packed a bag for the two of us, rung Paul, rung Mum, and arrived at the Royal Free Hospital.

We were seen immediately. The admissions nurse opened the letter Dr Grossmark had given to me and my heart nearly stopped dead when I saw the words 'suspected meningitis'. This had never been discussed; it had never occurred to me that we might be knocking at this particular door.

The hospital was fantastic, and soon, not just one, but three doctors of varying specialities were poring over my beloved baby. Thankfully, Max's listlessness that had so alarmed the GP had dissipated and he was grinning at all the attention. By the time Paul arrived, it was very clear the meningitis scare had slunk back into a dim and distant corner. The relief was indescribable.

Dr Epen did not give up on her attempts to cajole me into giving up my meagre helping of booze each day, but something soon happened that would. Still, her words induced guilt and thus I managed to reduce my consumption to a miniature bottle a day, similar to the ones provided on airplanes. I appeared to be managing my depression, although I still alternated between bleak and good periods. There were times when I saw the world for its profound beauty, could enjoy the simple magic of the stars on a cold, clear winter's night and feel optimistic about the coming day.

But these were muddled with episodes of despair, frustration, and if I'm being honest, rage. I was still bemoaning my bad luck, still asking why me? And so I suppose the act of ignoring Dr Epen's advice to stop drinking was also my way of saying, 'you can't take all my fun'. She dealt with me patiently, using facts not emotions in her attempts to persuade me. She told me how alcohol works as a depressant and that its effect is cumulative over a short period of time. I heard what she was saying loud and clear and I knew she was right – technically – but I still couldn't stop.

By now Max was receiving visits from an impressive team of therapists. My days were more or less structured around these. They were always tinged with disappointment and sadness, as it became painfully obvious how delayed Max really was. This feeling was exacerbated by watching Rachel's daughter Daisy develop and thrive, even though I know that Rachel never intended me to feel like this. At the time Rachel's friendship more than compensated for my constant comparisons. We spent many days together, enjoying the sunshine in the back garden, or solving the problems of the world around the kitchen table. The fact that Rachel was attuned to children with special needs provided me with a basic education and valuable insights into their world.

I remember one afternoon when Max was screaming with irritation. I was feeding him a fromage frais, as he was propped up on pillows in his highchair. That day I was having trouble coping with his irritation and accompanying wails until Rachel calmly informed me that Max was clearly cross with the colour of his spoon. I was feeding him his dessert with a blue spoon while Daisy had a red one. It was simple: he wanted a red spoon. Sure enough, as soon as I swapped blue with red, he gurgled with contentment and finished the lot.

That small observation made me realise how out of my depth I was. I was constantly underestimating Max, and had so much to learn, not least that I should never overlook the obvious. While I was frustrated I also knew that Max was a bright spark, determined and strong. He was an engaging baby who knew instinctively how to flirt and his ability to use his charm on people has never let up.

In terms of development the baby and childhood years of someone with DS are full of the same milestones and goals as any other child, only massively delayed. Rolling over, sitting up, walking and talking, all come eventually, some requiring more encouragement than others. The delays are years, rather than months and the older the child is, the more conspicuous the gap between a person with DS and their peers becomes. Some goals, including independent living and driving a car, may never be achieved. However, others such as getting married, having sex and an addiction to Bingo are all possible. People with Down's syndrome are individuals with their own gifts and personality traits who also happen to have a genetic defect. How they deal with the manifestations of this will depend quite significantly on their personality. Compared to a shy child, Max's outgoing, vibrant personality can only be an advantage, because to have the ability to interact with others will greatly accelerate his social skills, as it has done.

*

Despite being informed by the genetic counsellor that we stood a one in a hundred chance of having another child with DS, we wanted to add to our family. Before we got married we always discussed having children, not just one child. We thought about the odds long and hard but decided that we would try for a baby and accept whatever we were blessed with, whatever package he or she came in.

A word about antenatal testing for DS is called for here. My personal view is that it is somewhat oversold to the point where many women see it as some form of insurance; a guarantee against all eventualities. It's not.

Many more babies than you'd imagine are born with some kind of special needs. Obviously this can range from relatively minor afflictions such as mild learning difficulties, speech impediments, webbed feet, dispraxia and dyslexia, to the more life-threatening and life-changing ones. However much our perfection-driven society would like it, life has no guarantees. Just because a test comes back as negative for one particular condition, it does not mean you are out of the woods. In a way DS has a label, a badge that immediately places it within identifiable parameters and sets it up as one of the things for pregnant women to fear most. But I have seen so many children with special needs that are far greater than Max's. These children have no label, there is no identifiable cause, and not the remotest comprehension of their condition.

Both Paul and I agreed that in our attempts for a second child there would be no antenatal testing and no talk of terminations. If our child was healthy and 'standard', then that would be wonderful. But if he or she happened to be born with DS or any other special needs, we were prepared to welcome that child with loving, open arms. With the decision firmly made, we started the process of making babies. Fortunately, I only have to wash Paul's socks to get pregnant and, true to form, it didn't take long to conceive.

Surprisingly we were saved from any heavy-handed advice or moral lectures from the medical profession. As part of our discussion before trying for a baby, we'd also agreed that we would forgo our annual holiday and use the money more wisely by going private for the birth. We knew much of the discomfort and hospital chaos I'd encountered when having Max was all about lack of funding and being short staffed. The actual care (let's set aside the archaic presumptions about DS) I had received was of a good standard – there was just not enough of it. I was too fragile to endure a second similar experience, plus we both wanted to feel more in control. Mindful of our views on having any tests, our GP recommended an obstetric consultant who turned out to be absolutely right for me.

To this day I have no idea what his personal views are regarding antenatal testing. All I can say is that he was supportive, clear thinking and calm throughout my entire pregnancy. We did have a scan at 27 weeks to prepare us for any possible defects – including DS – our baby may have. As far as possible we wanted the birth to be a wonderful moment that we could enjoy for what it was.

Throughout my pregnancy I continued to make regular visits to Dr Epen. These therapy sessions now became an increasingly valuable support mechanism particularly as I was trying hard to keep a firm grip on my imagination. My therapy now became a place where I could moan about a process – pregnancy – that I cannot admit to relishing. I know there are women who love being pregnant but I'm not one of them and it has nothing to do with Max's birth. I hated it before he was born. For me it's a constant battle where you feeling disgustingly sick, drained of energy and not in control of your body. Unfortunately I didn't experience the romance and warm glow that some people attach to it.

For those nine months Dr Epen managed to steer me towards a sensible path of dignified control. While there were many times when I was cranky and fearful, I was also optimistic. I am aware that it's easy to say so now, but I had such a positive feeling about the child I was carrying. With Max I always had the underlying worry that something was wrong: this time, it was quite the opposite. I could finally understand the moans of other women whose little bundles were keeping them awake at night with their overzealous kicking and wriggling. Our baby – who we now knew was another boy – would rummage about in my stomach, rather like it was a deep, cavernous handbag and he was desperately searching for his keys.

It wasn't all plain sailing. At one point we received a comment so insensitive and patronising I am seething with anger even as I write this. A friend was out watering her garden as Paul and I were taking an evening walk. My bump was quite obvious by now and on seeing the two of us strolling along with Max in his pushchair she exclaimed with delight. But her reaction to my pregnancy was both cold and cruel.

'We are so pleased that you and Paul are going to have another baby,' she had said. 'Now you will be able to experience what it's really like to be a parent.'

Those words stung and continued to hurt long afterwards when you're still searching for appropriate replies. At the same time there is a sense of disbelief that somebody actually said that. Perhaps I was mistaken? Or misheard? Sadly I hadn't; the message had been delivered loud and clear. Was that how most people viewed our child? Did others view us as being left out in the wilderness, making do with pretend parenting? Did we really evoke such condescending pity? To me it was incredible that not only could anyone think such vile rubbish but that they could not stop themselves from verbalising it.

My pregnancy progressed and within only a few months, I was rather enormous. This continued until I reached my ninth month when I was, frankly, terrifying to the naked eye. Two weeks before the baby was due my stomach was a protrusion of mammoth proportions and everyone, me included, began to worry about two things. Firstly, that because my first labour was so rapid, it was highly likely that my second would also be relatively speedy. And then, if we left my baby to cook for another two weeks getting him out would be a nightmare. To my delight and relief they recommended that I be induced. The conversation Paul and I had with my consultant is still vivid in my memory. He was mulling over his diary, pondering on when best to invite me in to hospital to perform the induction. (I would have cheerfully hopped on to the nearest vacant bed, and popped my baby out there and then.) Instead he graciously suggested I come along to the Lindo Wing of St Mary's Hospital, Paddington, on the following Saturday – obviously grouping all his 'induction' ladies into one controllable day. Much to his bemusement, I promptly burst into tears.

'It's only four days' time, Mrs Lewis.'

'It may be four days to you, but it's a lifetime to me,' I protested.

It was the middle of August; I was the size of a small ocean liner, my baby was growing rapidly by the hour, and his exit route looked increasingly implausible. The four days dragged slowly past, my mum moved in to look after Max and, finally, Paul and I headed for the hospital. I would have jogged there, I was that keen.

From the outset, the approach to this birth was significantly different to Max's. We were calm, prepared and in control. They induced me, gave me an epidural and two hours later Charlie Angus Sinclare Lewis presented himself to the world: a perfectly healthy baby boy. Looking down at him, not 10 seconds old, I was amazed at his size. Not only was he big boned and muscular, but he was also very long. The idea that, moments earlier, he was tucked up inside my tummy astonished me.

I was so relieved to finally hold Charlie in my arms. Almost immediately I realised that he was so similar to Max, even without the DS. While I was pregnant, one thing I'd fretted over was finding extra love for him and where exactly it would come from. I worried about having to divide my love between the two boys and wondered if I would have enough for both of them. My concerns were unjustified as I soon discovered a second child brings with it more love and an increased capacity to give love.

It took me days to fully believe that Charlie did not have DS. Even though I had a sneaking suspicion throughout my pregnancy that he was going to be fine I hardly dared admit this to myself for fear of invoking a curse over his birth. I had almost made myself believe that Charlie also having DS would be the only outcome to expect. I was so prepared to welcome my newborn with DS, that it made it very difficult for me to fathom that he didn't.

It's difficult to put into words how I felt after the birth of Charlie without appearing to compare him to Max. I never have and never will. They are two dramatically different individuals. Nonetheless I wish Charlie had come first so I could have experienced – without any encumbrance – the exquisite joy and sheer pride you feel at the birth of your first child. When I held Charlie in my arms, a glow of optimism and delight surrounded us. I had no nagging worry gnawing me inside. Good or bad I could be blissfully unaware of what lay ahead for him. In short, I didn't have to think beyond that moment. With Max there was love, for sure there was love. But there was also worry and uncertainty that meant I couldn't enjoy that moment to its fullest.

Having Charlie empowered me: I could now see with my own eyes, understand with my own mind, all there was to know about a 'normal' baby and I felt reassured because I saw there is no difference. That knowledge gave me strength. I was no longer a poor excuse for a mother. I could now raise my head high and rebut all those people who'd levelled at me the charge of not understanding real motherhood. Having Charlie enabled me to click all my armour into place. I no longer felt vulnerable, as if I was someone who could evoke only pity.

I felt no different towards either one of my sons, but it made me feel very different towards everyone else.

Chapter Eight

3 October

Came back from a birthday party for my nephew Will today, he was three, what a poppet. His party had a nautical theme, so I made Max a cute little sailor's outfit, topped off with a blue-and-white pixie hat; he looked so gorgeous. Mandy living in Barnes is so near, yet so far. I do wish we lived closer. Great to see her though, and Will and Fraser. The party was full of typical well-off, south London mums. Very nice, but very privileged. I did well, all things considered. I managed to remain upbeat and chirpy, even though the odds were stacked against me. The whole house was full of loud, healthy, robust toddlers.

I wondered how many of the mums were aware of me and Max. Did they make the connection that Mandy and I were sisters and that Max had DS? I guess the unspoken risk of attention put me on edge, but I tried to smile all the way through, too much perhaps. Plus Mandy was lovely, I feel very safe in her company. The torturous event finally came to an end and Max and I had survived all the noise and the chaos and the mayhem. I faked huge enjoyment, but left early, with the excuse that I had had to allow plenty of time to miss the rush-hour traffic on the North Circular. Got home, only to find I had lost my Filofax. I thought I must have left it at Mandy's, so I rang to check. She couldn't find it; I guess the stress of losing it must have tipped me over the edge, because I completely lost my carefully moulded composure. I started to sob down the phone, muttering about Max never being the same as all those kids today. Never having the same blessed future or opportunity in life they will take for granted. This just fills me with such sadness. Bless her, she did her best, but was stumped for a worthy reply. God, I feel so stupid, such a victim, which I'm not. Being a victim does not sit well with me; I hate it, but I can't shrug off the conse-quences of Max's birth, the impact it will have not just on his life, but on all of us.

My family was now complete. I was unwilling to push my luck further and I couldn't abide being pregnant so I liked the idea that it was all done with. I honestly fail to understand how mothers cope with more than two children. To hold down a full-time job as well as juggling a busy household is completely beyond me, and the women who do have my utmost respect and admiration. My two little baby boys were more than I could hope for and, quite frankly, manage. In an attempt to stay ahead of the game I developed strict routines. They didn't always work but I told myself that at least I was trying.

When I first had Charlie, I enlisted the help of Helen and her daughter, Gemma. They regularly came to help me out with Max, taking him to the park and entertaining him, which gave me time to coax Charlie into a decent routine and also to recover from the grim task of giving birth. I was so fortunate to have such friends around. The birth of Charlie had left me feeling so mentally strong that I wrote to Dr Epen to tell her I did not need to attend any more sessions for the foreseeable future. I felt I had gained the strength to battle though my illness alone. How wrong I was.

Two children under the age of three is a big task even if one of them does not have DS. I certainly had my work cut out. Max appeared to bond well with his new brother, although he did go through a brief period of what I can only describe as depression, where he became quiet and withdrawn. He had realised he was not the only focus of our affection any more and that he had to share us with a smaller person who was very loud. To his credit he came through it and soon bounced back to his robust chirpy self.

Both Max and Charlie quickly made it known that they were prepared to jostle for any attention that was going. Their individual skills and talents in doing so knew no bounds. I found it quite unnerving to see how innovative and clever such little humans could be. It wasn't as if Paul and I didn't lavish attention on both of them: we did it constantly and we made them our entire world. They had me to themselves all day long and then they had Paul first thing in the morning and all weekend but still they wanted more of the spotlight.

One of the activities I came to dread most was going to the park. For a young child this part of the day is often heaven, but for me it was hell as I had to constantly endure the idle stares of people. They would glance at us and then look back again, unable to control themselves. I hated it. I hated having to brace myself for what I might attract. I know that some people reading this – those of thicker skin – may be wondering why I go on about this so much.

I wish it didn't hurt. I wish I could have just brushed it off but I couldn't and I still can't. The looks would settle first on Max. Having figured out that he had DS they would quickly fall on me and then flick back to

Max. Maybe there would be a cursory stare at Charlie, but of course it was Max they lingered on. Sometimes the need for verbal inquiry would seize them and, unable to display any sign of decent manners, or perhaps oblivious to their intrusion, they would come out with comments like: 'Are you the nanny? You don't look old enough to have a child with Down's syndrome. Will he grow out of it?' I began to resent and dread the reactions we received on these visits to the park. The knowledge that we were likely to provoke such a reception wherever we went, created a huge barrier even before we'd got past the front door.

Instead of rising to that challenge I chose to be private, to hide away from the questions and stares. I created my own park in our garden. I don't think my children suffered; they had a fantastic miniature park all of their own. We still visit green, lush, woodland parks but thankfully never again will I have to face those ominous slides, swings and seesaws that had become so sinister.

Max was now two and half and while his cheery personality, along with a love for bread and vanilla ice cream, was thriving, there were still the persistent battles with his health. Fighting off viruses throughout the winter and most of the summer was a constant worry. He also developed a distressing weakness for brutal attacks of croup. From nowhere a cold would develop into a barking seal-like cough, which would send us all into a state of sheer panic. Croup is a result of the throat constricting. In an adult this would present itself in the loss of voice but in a baby or child it's a high-pitched, barking cough. Children do grow out of it, usually around the age of seven or eight, but until then it can be worrying. Max's croup would always arrive at around 11 o'clock at night. Just when we thought he was sleeping peacefully and had another wretched cold under control, that familiar barking would start, indicating his inability to breathe fully. We would spend many panicky hours long into the night, worried to the point of insanity. A bathroom full of hot steam is thought to help so we tried it, but its effect on Max was relatively minimal. There were times when the croup was so bad that Max would end up in the back of an ambulance, attached to a nebuliser as we took him to hospital.

I soon began to search for some different approaches to Max's health, not as a replacement to conventional medicine, but as additional support to help us through these situations. One such alternative was homeopathy. I had been familiar with it for some time, and felt comfortable with some of the results it could achieve. In fact, just after Max was born I experienced it for myself.

I had been a new mother for just a few weeks when my entire left arm began to swell, preventing me from even attempting to bend it. I took myself to casualty where the doctor discovered a small lump on my finger, just beneath the skin. On closer examination with a needle it seemed it was full of something nasty and he suggested it was the origin of a potentially hazardous infection.

It must have been serious since he recommended that I be placed on an antibiotic drip in hospital for up to a week. The thought of being in hospital with a tiny newborn baby for any duration of time, never mind the estimated week, was just completely beyond what I could accept. I did not disagree with the diagnosis but I couldn't face going into hospital. It took some persuading, but I convinced them to let me go home so that I could organise myself and Max for our return the next morning. On the way home I rang my homeopath, and she agreed to see me. She gave me a remedy, which I took there and then, and repeated for the next few hours. By morning, I was absolutely delighted to see that the swelling in my arm had gone down considerably. By the end of the day my arm was almost back to normal. A quick phone call to the hospital cancelled my stay and I was over the moon. I do not for one minute suggest that a conventional approach would not have worked in the same way, but this route was far more palatable.

I stayed quiet about going to see a homeopath for Max's croup because I didn't want to deal with the inevitable objections I'd get from various people who didn't understand it. The homeopath gave me aconite; a remedy she suggested would work well for attacks of croup. It proved a lifesaver. As soon as Max presented us with his baby seal-like barking, I gave him the tiny pills of aconite and his croup stopped dead in its tracks. No steamy bathroom, no panic, no ambulance, just a baby with no barking cough. He would still endure a vicious cold, but no croup. From then on I turned increasingly to alternative approaches to help support Max's health. Conventional medicine still played a very large and important part: however, I complemented it with the help of homeopathy, cranial osteopathy, and reflexology.

I remember when both the boys had chicken pox. Charlie appeared with a face full of spots one morning; he clearly had chicken pox and was mildly ill for a few days. Luckily he was able to battle off the invasion without too much bother. Ten days later Max went down with such large blistering, weeping spots that I couldn't help but wince just looking at him. He was in agony and experiencing a trauma no child should endure. He was given antibiotics to prevent the spots from turning septic and posing a threat to the hole in his heart, but apart from these, there was very little the doctors could do to ease his discomfort.

In desperation I asked Janet Prower, a cranial osteopath, if she would see him. Max lay on her treatment couch writhing in agony, moaning and crying with pain. Within a few minutes Janet had massaged his head and I saw him uncurl like a cat, relax and fall asleep. She worked on him for a further half an hour and I carried my sleeping child to the car, returning him home to his cot. He slept for the next 10 hours and awoke, having arrived at a turning point in his illness. From then on he continued to recover from the chicken pox and regain good health. A powerful vision for me, one I can't explain, but quite frankly feel no desire to.

With Max's croup now relatively under control, we decided to attempt a family holiday with our two children. We flew to Cyprus for two weeks. To describe any break away from home with young children as a holiday is a contradiction in itself. However, although the day-to-day maintenance of our children was a challenge, we did enjoy the benefits an organised holiday could bring. It was refreshing to be away from the low-grade, persistent guilt that effortlessly plagued me regarding Max's therapy. Again, we were forced to tolerate the stares but we also discovered different attitudes to DS. Rather disarming displays of kindness were often afforded to us, which left me confused. In some cases the overzealous kindness could be explained because a member of their own family had perhaps been touched by similar circumstances. Or maybe, from time to time, you just miraculously stumble across people with no hidden agenda who genuinely express warmth and consideration wherever they are. We have always accepted these kindnesses with good grace; however, it can be highly embarrassing for Charlie. He never attracts such attention when he goes out – thank goodness, because he is particularly shy – but from an early age he must have questioned such bizarre behaviour towards his older brother. For him, Max is his brother, a pain in the arse just like any sibling can be and that's how he sees him.

On this holiday it was Charlie's turn to strike his own memorable chord in history. He behaved in such an outrageous manner that he almost got us thrown out of the hotel, which is not bad for an 11-month-old.

We were all sleeping peacefully one night when Charlie awoke. He decided he no longer wanted to be in his cot, even though it was the middle of the night and we had made it clear to him he had to sleep. It was like a chemical reaction. BOOM! Off he went into an explosion that lasted for about half an hour. There was no reasoning or cajoling, no threats or flirting to bring him round. He screamed at the top of his lungs and no matter what we did he just would not shut up. I had him squawking over my shoulder when the telephone in the room rang. I picked up the receiver and a man said, 'Madam, your baby is crying.'

'Gosh,' I replied, 'I would never have realised.'

It took Paul ages of walking up and down the bedroom with Charlie in his arms for this angry young creature to come to the end of his first temper tantrum. The following morning at breakfast, as I strapped my baby into his highchair, I felt deeply embarrassed knowing full well he was the reason for all the bleary eyes and tired faces surrounding us.

As I write, all these years later, I can see only too clearly that this first tantrum was a sign of things to come. Charlie's temper is a big part of him; explosive and fascinating to watch (as well as a bloody nuisance). Thankfully, now that he's nearly 12 he is more in control of it. But it's always there.

Chapter Nine

15 August

I am gobsmacked and have an inner rage like no other. Other human beings never fail to astonish me. Some of them stun me with their utter lack of charm and humility. Today we were driving into a car park, just outside of Padstow in Cornwall, me, Paul, the boys in the back. The ticket man came over to my window all smiles, as I gave him the money. Whilst handing me my ticket, along with my change, he cheerfully asked me the following, and I quote, 'How come you had him then?' (Nudges head in Max's direction.) 'Aren't there tests you can do these days? You being so young, love, such a shame.'

I was speechless and appalled. My sons were in the back of the car and yet this man saw no problem in engaging in such an unforgivable conversation in front of them, never mind the fact that Max, yet again, must endure such openly disgusting remarks *about his very existence. I wanted to drown this man very slowly in acid, but remarkably I managed to ignore him. Charlie then piped up from the back, 'What a bad man.'*

When Charlie was approaching three I decided to look for a nursery for him. He was a demanding little chap and I felt that some degree of exposure to other children would do him the world of good. Rachel had recommended a great nursery in Hampstead Garden Suburb called Speedwell, which was held in a local tennis pavilion. She had heard great things about it, so I applied for both the boys to go. By this time Max had been going to his nursery in Hendon for some two years, and whilst I was hesitant to make any change, I wanted my children to attend the same nursery, to be together like any other young siblings. I wanted them to enjoy a childhood, however brief, where I could delude myself that we lived in an idyllic world.

The nursery was run by a warm, spirited lady called Abigail. Not only was she welcoming and supportive towards Charlie, but she also showed tremendous warmth and respect towards Max on our visit. You can never be entirely sure about the impression you get from an individual, and I am particularly inept at spotting complete nutcases, but I knew that my children would be safe in Abigail's hands from the moment we met.

It was there that I met a mother of two little girls in the first week of term. Louise was very friendly and I warmed to her immediately. One of her daughters, Bonnie, had shown a particular affection towards Max, and Louise invited both my boys to Bonnie's birthday tea the following week. This was the first bit of real inclusion I had encountered within the rocky world of preschool mother and toddlers and I was so grateful towards her for the gesture. Not once had Max been invited for tea with a friend at his previous nursery. As luck would have it, we couldn't go, but I made certain to extend the invite by inviting them to ours a few days later. I made a little birthday cake and the four children had an exclusive tea party all of their own.

Louise had a great sense of humour and we immediately clicked. Her kindness also touched me, and I think the two of us, for very different reasons, desperately needed a friend at that particular time in our lives. With our children happy to play in one another's company, our friendship blossomed. I was delighted that she worked so hard at being my friend. Nobody had ever gone to such lengths to make me feel special and needed. I loved it and it was a tremendous gift at a very difficult time in my life. We would see each other every morning at the nursery and Louise would always coax me into having a coffee with her in a local café. I've never started the day enjoying a simple cup of coffee with a friend so this was a total luxury. We spent such a large part of our time together laughing, again something I had not managed for a very long time. We would invariably meet after the children had finished their morning at the nursery and would end up in one another's homes, drinking tea and watching our children playing and growing before our very eyes.

Max and Charlie took to the nursery well and, although I was still very raw and sensitive to anybody's reaction to Max, those years were full of fun. They were probably the last few months of Max's childhood when I could kid myself that he was almost the same as everybody else. His personality was so colourful that he broke hearts wherever he went. On leaving the nursery in Hendon, I was told by Helen that he was one of the most memorable personalities they had ever encountered. I can only agree as I've seen with my own eyes the effect he has on people. He draws the best from everyone and rewards them for their attention with his sparkling eyes and adorable giggle. Their hearts would just melt.

I was more comfortable leaving Max at the nursery than Charlie. Max is a survivor and uses what skills he has tremendously efficiently. He has this knack of getting people to run around for him, helping him with things he's often more than capable of doing himself, but he rewards them tenfold.

Louise and I became so close that Paul and I made the unusual step of agreeing to go on a joint family holiday to Portugal. We had a great time; Louise and her husband Alex were very understanding and accommodating over every irritating compromise we had to make in consideration of Max. Their children Bonnie and Lily got on tremendously well with our boys; they were all under the age of four and were content with the plentiful supply of sunshine and ice creams. Their little family unit seemed far more tranquil and calm than our own because they did not have the added complication of Max's needs. On occasions it served as a rude awakening for me and Paul.

Max still couldn't walk or talk and got by the best he could. He had many tantrums at that time, and in hindsight I can see they were due to fear of a new situation and his unspeakable rage at not being able to make us understand him. I now know he enjoys routine and anything that disrupts his status quo confuses and terrifies him. Paul and I felt for him and at the same time we envied other families we would spot on the beach. We still do.

Louise and I returned from holiday firm friends. I laughed most of the time I was with her. She was outrageous and cheeky to a degree I could only dream of. I think we drew a mutual sense of security from our friendship. We provided each other with confidence that enabled us to cope with the perils of motherhood and the rubbish life chucks at you.

As always, another brief period of calm waters was to be interrupted. Max had to be admitted to the Eastman Dental Hospital for some extensive dental work. We knew it was coming, but that didn't make it any easier when it arrived. We worried about everything: the anaesthetic, the operation, Max's recovery. It all merged into one big knot in my stomach and I constantly felt nauseous. We arrived at the Eastman wishing we were anywhere but there.

We were directed to the children's ward, and I found it hard to stay upbeat. Yet the staff were fantastic, all of them true professionals and so kind to us, especially to Max. They immediately rose to the challenge of handling him in the least stressful way. He had to have antibiotic cover before and after the operation. There is a direct connection between the teeth and the heart, and with Max's hole this was of particular concern. Whenever Max has any dental work, he always has to have antibiotic cover, and runs a small risk of serious heart complications if he should develop any unchecked infection or abscess in his mouth. He was placed first on the operating list, so his waiting time would be minimal. I was preoccupied with the notion that he would fail to come around from the anaesthetic, or that they would accidentally drop debris down his throat and he would choke to death. I was handing over the control and care of my child to people who didn't even know him, which I found very hard to do.

When Max was checked over there was some concern that he had a cold. He always had a cold; it was almost impossible to find a window when he was cold-free. But an anaesthetic can only be given to a fully fit child. The decision was agony; part of me wanted them to say, 'no, not today I'm afraid', but the other part of me wanted to get it over and done with. In the end, they felt that they could cope with the extra phlegm, and he was not spiking a temperature, so I agreed to go ahead.

By far the worst moment was putting him to sleep. The procedure was intimidating for all of us, but Max was truly frightened, even though I will say the staff did everything in their power to make the procedure as calm as possible. As usual they couldn't find a vein in his hand to stick in the needle, and it ended up in his foot.

That made me feel sick and I just couldn't hold back my tears. Mercifully he was asleep in seconds, and I reluctantly had to let him go.

It was an agonising wait, but he was actually in and out of the operating theatre relatively quickly. They called us as soon as he came out of the operation, and we knew everything was fine when we saw his eyes open. When he saw the Barney video I was holding up for him, he gave us a huge smile. We'd bought it in readiness for after his operation; it was intended to be a big apology for what we had put him through. He had had four fillings and a stainless steel crown. With Max's mouth at her disposal the dentist also took the opportunity to coat all his teeth in the resin used to help prevent decay. All this and he was still only on his baby teeth. With Max discharged you'd think we were over the moon. But we weren't.

We never are. Sure, there's relief, but it's the relief of soldiers who've returned from battle, weary and exhausted. Plus there's the knowledge that it will all happen again because that's the way things are now. If you live on the edge of a drama, constantly on your guard, then you never forget; you are always fully prepared for 'fight or flight'. And that adrenalin comes at a high price. Your body is always in stress mode. The bottles of wine felt like they helped – they certainly dulled the impact of the experience and gave a brief respite from the trauma – but realistically alcohol was just a sticking plaster, and not a terribly good one at that.

Chapter Ten

16 August

Today we endured another visit to the community paediatrician. I am still left bemused each time we visit. We go simply because we are told we must. Although nothing really comes out of these appointments, apparently if we don't attend, Max will somehow stop developing properly. Yes, it is ridiculous.

He's measured and weighed and it's noted. He's given these tests which mean he's judged mercilessly in a five-minute time slot. His whole IQ level seems to be dependent on these few precious moments. He's told to make a tower from three blocks and then given a black mark when he refuses to bash them over after, as instructed, he adds a fourth. Creatively speaking I'm not sure I'd be tremendously keen on having to sabotage my painstakingly crafted work, not to mention just not wanting to comply with authority. We always come away feeling dreadfully defeated, and I never fail to cry. I guess it's a system of sorts; it allows the big bureaucratic machine to monitor him. When I gather the courage I think we shall stop going. I have no idea when that will be.

I used to scoff when I heard older people say, 'blink and their childhood will be gone' or 'they grow up so quickly'. They're right. Suddenly I was faced with the daunting prospect of sending Max to school. Paul and I never even considered a special school for him. From the outset we were determined that he should go to a mainstream school. Our next logical thought was to place him in the very best regular school we could find. We never paused to think that perhaps in striving for a primary school of such excellent reputation, we would be among parents who were determined to see their own children excel academically. There is nothing fundamentally wrong with this; after all, every parent strives for the absolute best for their children, Paul and myself included. However, if we'd been able to take just a small step back and think logically, we may have seen that our desire to gain access to such a competitive environment would be setting our son up for a monumental fall. But you don't think like that, do you? You think of the positives, imagining that this is the environment where your little one will thrive and prosper, no matter what their abilities.

I have no doubt that it was a fantastic school. The staff was dedicated, enthusiastic and experienced. They were headed by Sheila Abbott, a formidable character. I'm tempted to describe her as a genius, because in many ways she was. Sheila took the possibility of Max entering her educational oasis completely in her stride. I still remember her initial reply to my tentative enquiry as to whether she would consider accepting my son at her school: 'If Brooklands is the place for Max to go to school, then Brooklands is the place he will be.'

Sheila invited herself around for tea. A petite, elegant woman stood on my doorstep one Friday afternoon, but her frame bore no resemblance to her qualities as a head teacher. Her strength, determination and unwavering directness left me slightly wobbly. I admit she scared the pants off me, something I never overcame. Sheila tolerated no fuss or silly nonsense in reaching her ambitious objectives. Not only did she rule with steel resolve, but she also underscored her leadership with charm and acute people skills. Nothing fazed her and I'm sure she would have succeeded at whatever profession she chose.

We felt so welcome at Brooklands that we drifted along with the charm and delight of it all. We could walk to school via pretty alleyways decorated with blossoming, lush green hedgerows. We'd greet little friends along our journey, all happy to be wearing the special, emerald-green polo shirts with the embroidered Brooklands logo. Such acceptance and normality was so enticing. We just wanted to be part of that dream full of opportunity and good fortune. Max was still a cute, overgrown toddler. The gap compared to his peers was there but blink and you could miss it if you wanted, which I did so very much.

With the gift of hindsight, I would have planned Max's education in a rather different way if I had the chance to do it all over again. I would have swallowed the forgivable desire for my child to attend the local school. Instead, I would have chosen a school with a good reputation, but free from middle-class, achievement-driven parents. It may have been in an area where English is perhaps not the first language for a substantial proportion of the children. That alone would have meant that Max was not automatically at the bottom of the food chain. If the school were situated in an area that serviced a local community that was not especially wealthy and competitively driven, Max may have stood a far better chance. It may have boosted his confidence and he may have felt more inclined to try harder, as he would not always be at the bottom of the class, far behind his peers. It strikes me as so obvious now, but I was so anxious and naive at the time. I was also in denial and that itself was enough for me to go along with the general consensus that all children with DS should be educated in mainstream schools. It's a good theory, but it requires serious financial commitment from the government, otherwise it is just a token social gesture. It also requires diligent care by the parents when it comes to selecting the school.

Today I have big regrets. Max fell through many nets both socially and educationally, all for my selfish dream of pretending he was 'normal'. For a child with special needs, surviving in a mainstream school is not necessarily normal; it can be sad. To thrive, a child must be supported and made to feel confident. Having DS and going to a mainstream school ultimately demonstrates to that individual child that they are not there to succeed. How can they, when at best they are drowned with kindness, and at worst tolerated? In these cases children with DS exist not on their own terms but on those of others since they are the ones who must work incredibly hard to try and feel like a bona fide member of the school, rather than being there as just a token nod towards inclusion. People with DS may have a low IQ but they are in no way stupid. They are perceptive and sensitive to other people's reactions and behaviour. They may not make a verbal fuss, or be capable of articulating their views fully, but they still exist passionately in the world.

Along the way Paul and I had many reminders of what a beast of a mountain we were trying to climb. We did a lot of pretending in those years, but sanity still prevailed when it came to coping with blatant abuse by certain professionals. Long before Max was due to attend school we paid for him to be assessed by a private educational psychologist. We felt it was worth the money, if only for the sensible suggestion that whatever we decided to do about Max's schooling, we should delay everything by a year. We also received a painful, but detailed, account of where our son was at in his development and so were under no illusion about his position in the learning tree. Just before Max started at Brooklands we were visited by an educational psychologist from the local authority. She needed to assess Max as a part of his entry into mainstream school.

It's a meeting that I will never forget: perhaps my memory is tinged with cynicism and I have to accept that organisations must look to the bigger picture when dealing with any issue, but it serves as a stark reminder to me when I'm lured into trusting anybody who may have other important agendas to consider alongside my son's welfare. It's savvy to assume that whoever comes into contact with Max in a professional capacity may have an additional agenda, unless we're paying them of course! I'm referring here to the education system, but any system is possibly the same. It may not always be the case and I'm not blaming individuals within the system: their job will always embrace broader issues than isolated claims, but in the end usually it's all about money; who's got it, who gives it out and who needs it. If you remember that important fact and focus in a very ice-cold, determined way, even if it may not be entirely the case, you can't go far wrong.

And so the local authority educational psychologist came to visit us one afternoon for tea. She appeared a dedicated, affable profesional who I'm convinced was quite genuine in her recommendations, but afterwards, when she had left, I couldn't help but feel sad. We had never met before and she therefore had no knowledge of Max. She recommended that we did *not* have him statemented. A statement of educational needs is a contract between the local education authority and the parents of a child with special needs. It is a legal document that states the support required, and how that support will be provided by the state. There is no downside for the parents in obtaining such a document but there is every downside for the state, since they are then legally bound to provide the designated support.

The educational psychologist felt that Max was doing well enough on his own. Her professional view was that the stigma of being statemented can lead to embarrassment and ridicule for a child, which she felt we would not choose for our son.

Her words left me stunned and breathless. If I had wanted to be in total denial of Max's condition, her comments would have been music to my ears. But, my desire to get Max into a mainstream school notwithstanding, I didn't want to be in total denial, and I wasn't. Moreover I knew Max's position in the academic world only too well, and her suggestion that he did not require structured and well-planned full-time support within Brooklands I considered bizarre. I pointed out to her that Max's condition was plastered all over his face for all to see, and did she really imagine a child with DS could embark upon mainstream school without suitably agreed support? Even with the limited experience I possessed, I was shocked.

Paul and I decided that we had no choice but to write to the local education authority requesting that Max have a statement of educational needs. By making our views very clear in a letter, we started the legal process. In truth the whole procedure became a formality. The professionals were perfectly aware that Max required considerable assistance and, within the six-week time frame, Max had his statement of educational needs. From then on, I suspect Paul and I were seen as troublemakers. In the coming years we would cause havoc, ending up in a ridiculously financially draining legal case, far removed from the idyllic dreams we had for our son's education.

Day one of school came around mightily quick. I couldn't believe we were among those little troopers skipping to school. Well, not skipping; the short walk was beyond Max, so he was in a pushchair, which was in itself a major giveaway. Although he was six years old, he was still in nappies and I wondered how he felt about having others realise pretty quickly that he was not quite up to their speed. Max has never been oblivious to his condition: he is only too aware that he has DS. How could he miss the stares? How could he not realise that his younger brother was more able than him? In fact, he had started to shout at people who stared at him in the street, demanding why their eyes crawled all over him. They soon shuffled quickly by on their journey, and I was very proud of him. Max was never a pushover. He has very clear views on how he perceives life and for me that is highly reassuring.

Max's first-ever teacher was a woman totally dedicated to her craft, Jaia Crebbin. I have never come across a more selfless individual. Her intuition was extraordinary and she really seemed to understand little people. Max spent two years with her in the 'Lions'. If only life could be like that class. The children saw no major difference in Max, not until their parents pointed it out to them. They were wrapped in generosity of spirit, cherished and encouraged to thrive. With his dynamic, affecting personality Max soon became well-known throughout the school. He appeared to cast a spell over most people he came into contact with, especially all the nursery nurses who had a higher than average involvement with him. These nurses – Wendy, Adrienne and Jan – succeeded in quashing most of my initial anxiety. Mike Catley was the classroom assistant and is still a good friend today, which in itself speaks volumes. He has such a way with all the children and like his colleagues, is truly gifted.

Another wonderful person to be around Max at this time was Jackie, a trained occupational therapist. Jackie immediately gave me tremendous reassurance. I knew that although she led Max to think he was the decision maker and in full control, she was gently guiding him in the right direction. She gave Max many gifts, not the material kind, but far more valuable ones, like self-respect and dignity.

It's important to emphasise how lucky we were to

have such good people around Max. Whilst thankfully I'm sure such cases are rare, there was one unfortunate incident for us, which occurred while we were on a week's break. Paul and I took the boys away on a last-minute bargain abroad, just for a few days; the credit card could handle it and we put all our faith into the saying 'a change is as good as a rest'.

When we arrived at the all-inclusive hotel we were impressed by everything especially the children's club, with its team of experienced English support staff. The boys were still toddlers, happy to draw, swim and generally muck about, so we saw no harm in letting them go to the club for an afternoon. The few hours we would have to ourselves were a strong incentive, and we thought they'd have fun.

When we picked them up at the end of the session a parent of another child who was also visiting the club approached us and tactfully related an incident he had witnessed that made him rather uncomfortable. It will always be etched on my memory. He said that while unintentionally hidden in the doorway waiting for his own child, he witnessed one of the carers being shockingly mean to Max, berating him angrily when he wet himself.

When you discover that an individual close to your child, who appears to be generous and warm, can in fact sometimes be cruel and short on tolerance, it is quite frightening. This is especially so when you have a child with special needs who cannot distinguish between acceptable and unacceptable behaviour or verbalise their feelings. Perhaps this young woman was unaware that her behaviour was unacceptable: after all, individuals can vary wildly in their nature, and maybe I'm being naive to assume that my son will always be met with overwhelming kindness. The carer's behaviour may have been completely unintentional, but to find out she was being unpleasant and mean to my son was chilling. Initially a small part of me wanted to dismiss this parent's accusation and enjoy a trouble-free life. But my priority as a mother was to protect my son.

We never returned to the children's club; we were only at the hotel for a week and we decided to treat the incident as just a bad memory, but that carer is still there today, lurking in the back of my mind. She's a reminder of everything a mother hates to think about, not least that a kind face may not always be what it appears. For the sake of your child, you owe it to them to always be three steps ahead of anyone whose care you place them in. Little people cannot speak up for themselves and those like Max even less so.

With a full academic year behind him, Max had become a permanent fixture at the school. His spirit and charm gained him entrance to many people's hearts, and I don't think it's being immodest or far-fetched to say the majority of the school and parents benefited from his presence. He taught them tolerance and humility and widened their view of the world. Did I relish the fact that my son enriched other people's lives in such a way? As a by-product of circumstances, I didn't mind.

Still, it was odd to know that his condition afforded us a strange kind of celebrity. It was soon very clear that I wasn't just another mother at the school gate: I was Max's mother. Because people knew who I was, I felt that I couldn't just jump out of bed, throw on the nearest clothes and do the school run. I didn't dare go out without make-up because I knew that people would be looking at me, at us. If it sounds like I felt I had an obligation to keep up appearances, then yes, I did. Everything we did was out of the ordinary: while other kids throwing tantrums was ignored, Max's tears were noticed. We were noticed. Everything with Max was that little bit different.

Chapter Eleven

15 July

I was out shopping with Max and Charlie yesterday. We bumped into someone I vaguely know from a book club I used to attend. The conversation went a bit like this:

CLAIRE: *Hi Sandy, how are you?*

ME: *Hi Claire, I'm fine thanks. How are you?*

CLAIRE: *Well, to be honest I'm not feeling so good, rather sick in fact; I'm pregnant.*

ME: *Congratulations! What lovely news.*

CLAIRE: *Actually I'm not regarding it as a viable pregnancy as yet. We certainly haven't told the boys.*

ME: *Oh?*

CLAIRE: *I'm over forty now and I'm not taking any chances. I'm still waiting for my AFP test to come back. Until that's okay I'm not viewing this as good news.*

ME: *I'm confused. What is an AFP test?*

CLAIRE: *A test for Down's syndrome! You of all people should know that!*

ME: *I see, well best of luck.*

I walked away, the tears prickling their way into my eyes.

If she had slapped me with the back of her hand, I doubt it would have stung as much. To say such a God-awful thing to anyone in public is bad enough, never mind to me, with Max running around in front of us. How chilling that she probably felt, as do many people, that this kind of conversation is perfectly socially acceptable. They might all smile broadly at my son and me, but behind the facade they are thanking their lucky stars that they're not me and their children aren't him. What a lovely reminder for them that their lives could be worse. I feel I'm almost providing a public service. I just wanted to come home, crawl under the sheets and howl. This world should get easier to deal with but it doesn't.

The year after Max started at Brooklands, his younger brother joined him. Max was then six and Charlie four. To have both my children at the same school felt a little bit magical to me. Max was to repeat the reception year and remain in the 'Lions' – which I was only too happy about. Jaia and Mike had developed such an empathy with Max, I felt like he was in the very best place for him. Charlie was to start in the 'Dolphins' class, another one of three classes within the reception year. As a mother it represented a brief yet delightful moment in time; one of those moments that make it all worthwhile.

Charlie's first day at school was a million miles away from Max's and not just because he does not have DS. Charlie is a sensitive, shy and somewhat cautious individual. He is not blessed with Max's natural charisma and appetite for attention. As I placed a final kiss on the top of his head, breathed in the sweet scent of chubby skin and waved him goodbye, he looked at me with fear and trepidation. Given the choice, I know he would have chosen to stay with me, just to be by my side. It wasn't that he hated going to nursery or disliked the thought of school; he just wasn't sure about things. And he was still remarkably young. Turning four in the summer holidays meant he was by far the youngest in his year. We had considered keeping him back, which was a possibility, but we were strongly advised not to wait. It would seem that Charlie had been fortunate to inherit serious brains, something that Paul and I were a little unprepared for. Up till now we had approached educational matters from the other end of the spectrum. To be faced with a child with high intelligence would be just as much of a challenge as one with special needs. From a very early age Charlie has been a very deep thinker, a bit too deep, really, because it almost disrupts his enjoyment of daily life. He also demonstrated the capacity to whip up a minor situation into something major in a nanosecond, and – as I've mentioned already – was equipped with a volatile temper to boot.

As a parent you wonder how you could have two children with markedly different personalities but that's the wonder of creation, I suppose. It's also a refreshing reminder that we are all individuals. Coping with the dramatically different needs of our sons proved a signif-icant strain and I often felt like I was caught between rival fans in a football stadium. For a start, it was very noisy so peace and tranquillity were luxuries. One would be screaming the place down with a hurt knee while playing in the garden, while the other would be trying to scoop out a terrified fish from the small aquarium we had in the lounge. Or one would need some help cutting up his lunch while the other would be running around with a dirty bottom. And both would need – and expect – immediate attention, preferably before the other! My children may sound like they are a couple of drama queens and like any children they can be too much to deal with on some days but, hey, that's part of the deal. They are like little lion cubs, exploring and discovering their place in the world.

I was very excited to have two little boys both wearing the same school jumper. Somehow this year I felt stronger because I could show people I had a regular son as well as a 'special' one. It was like saying, 'See, I can do it too.' I suppose I was hoping that instead of sympathy, people would show the same emotions they showed to each other and each other's children. I know it sounds contradictory, but now I hid behind Charlie; he made me feel whole and complete. Charlie struggled to settle in at school in those first few months but I never saw him rely on his older brother, even for reassurance. As far as I could tell he kept well away from him. Because the children were so young, they never asked Charlie about Max; that came later.

I believe now that I had underestimated how much Max would miss his former classmates. Yet again he tripped me up, displaying emotions I had failed to even consider. He knew there was a reason why he remained in the 'Lions' but he never challenged it. He saw his old friends in their new class with their new teacher, but being trapped in his prison of limited verbal communication, he was unable to ask why or talk through how he felt. We explained it to him the best we could, but in hindsight I'm not sure it was enough. His teacher, Jaia, understood exactly what was going on, so she did all the right things to make him feel important and valued. She asked him if he would mind helping her with the new children, suggesting that because he was such an experienced member of the 'Lions' his contribution to the day-to-day running of the class was invaluable.

He rose to the challenge and in doing so demonstrated patience and kindness towards his peers. It was also the one and only time where he got to experience how it feels to be king. But in truth, this was just a small sticking plaster over a gaping wound and his peers soon caught on to the daily routine and challenges of school life. Once again Max was left behind, struggling to join in with his new friends' games and chatter.

Because Max was the only one with DS in Brooklands, he was so isolated, and we had nobody to compare him to. We had no regular access to other children of a similar age with DS. He was probably doing as well as his peers with DS, but even now, when he has more contact with friends with DS, the range of abilities and talents is so vast, that it's hard to get a solid benchmark for any comparison.

Max's limited speech capability was a constant worry to us. Since his birth we had done all we could to encourage him to talk. He had regular speech therapy and we are a naturally communicative family, which I am sure helped. Within our private walls Max had no trouble making himself understood. We were all tuned into him and I would safely estimate that I understood 95 per cent of what he said. He would become very annoyed if we failed to understand him, but with a bit of lateral thinking, we managed to work out the extra five per cent most of the time.

The outside world was quite another matter. People would visibly struggle to understand him. Naturally this would cause them major embarrassment and Max would feel isolated and angry. The time had come to search for more help.

We found it through the wisdom and calm of Lyndsey, a speech and language therapist who had been recommended to us. Lyndsey was one of those people who was always smiling and Max immediately took to her. She looked slightly bohemian with a long black mane of hair, tied back in a swishing ponytail. Most of all, she was optimistic. One of the first things she ever said to me was that she had no doubt that Max would learn to speak; in fact, she felt that in time we would find it hard to get him to shut up. She was absolutely right!

Extra therapy came at a price and such financial burdens have increased as the years have passed. The sad fact is money does give you the freedom to seek out the best assistance; the more you have, the more doors will open for you. I sometimes fantasise about what great heights Max could reach had we unlimited funds. But not everything was about money. About the time when we were starting to make a major financial outlay on Max's development, Paul came to a dramatic life-changing decision in terms of his career. Paul is passionate about his family. It may have been a reaction to his own childhood, which was fraught with problems, but he has a dedication to us that is sometimes beyond comprehension to the outside world. It has always been his priority to be there for his children, and he puts them at the centre of everything in the strong belief that you 'reap what you sow'. I think he's right but it's not an attitude that is shared by everyone, especially employers. While some employers are well known for espousing family-friendly qualities, the truth is very few of them actually do something about it, especially for men. Moreover, the bosses of anyone in a position that is senior enough and well-paid enough will expect blood; in today's environment it's a given.

Paul's employers were no different. I'm not being biased when I say Paul is the perfect employee: he's accurate, focused, clever and perceptive and does not accept failure as an option. He gave his all to his job. He wasn't looking to do less work; he was looking for flexibility. You'd expect that, in our computer age, companies would be able to cope with that, especially from a trusted, high-performing employee, but they just couldn't get their heads around the idea. It was silly really, especially since much of Paul's work involved report writing at his computer or talking on the telephone. He could easily do much of his job from home, meaning he could choose when to work, and be on hand to support us when we needed him.

He spent a lot of time dealing with America and by allowing him this flexibility he could be readily available to them by working late into the night, during the American daytime. Likewise, in the morning, he could be at his desk at seven, wiping out all urgent enquiries and smoothing over any issues that had arisen from America overnight. With this small degree of flexibility, he would be able to see his children, take them to school a few times a week and be with them before they went to bed. It would mean I would have another adult on call. Although it seemed like a win-win solution for all concerned, Paul just couldn't seem to make his employers understand the benefits of this added flexibility. Eventually, Paul took the decision to resign. It wasn't easy for him: it took strength of character, since he was giving up an extremely well-paid job and the status that type of job confers on you. Lots of people thought he was completely mad and couldn't understand why he did it. In the end his departure could have been more amicable, but perhaps that's indicative of the life he was trying to escape.

What Paul did took guts. Giving up the cosy life of the employed and joining the consultants of this world can be a bleak and lonely place. You kiss goodbye to your company pension and expense account and learn to embrace lean times and anxiety. On the other hand, you gain a certain degree of control.

Just because Paul gave up the security and comfort of a massive company doesn't mean he slacked off. I have never seen him relaxing around the house drinking endless cups of coffee and wasting time. He works just as hard, if not harder. He's still in the movie business and he's always chasing something, finishing a report or completing a deal. I won't lie: it has been tremendously hard on occasions but such a display of strength and commitment from Paul more than makes up for any hardship. We now have considerably less money, but no regrets. Our children, although they will never perhaps realise it or thank us, have had Paul in their lives much more than they would have, had he stayed a company man.

One of the great benefits of Max becoming a consultant was that he didn't have to travel so frequently. The impact of the extensive travel his work demanded was a tremendous strain. Max in particular couldn't bear for Paul to go away and would literally pine for his return. But now Paul knows everything about his children, every inch of them, because he's always around. The first thing they ask when they see me is, 'Where's Dad?' What a tribute to him, an irreplaceable gift from father to sons. It's not as if I feel left out; I know I am loved and cherished because they often tell me, and it's never occurred to me to question my sons' devotion to their father. My own father has always been a huge influence and support to me. I've always been a 'daddy's girl' and to see such an affection duplicated by my sons, particularly by Max, seems so natural. No one can explain why children sometimes migrate towards one particular parent; it's very common, but exceptionally special.

Chapter Twelve

11 July

It's Saturday and I woke this morning to high-pitched squeals of delight coming from the kitchen. I crept down the stairs still in the throes of sleep, dragging my dressing gown around my nightie and paused to crouch on the last step, not wanting to break the spell.

I peered through the wooden banisters to see Paul in his flamboyant checked boxer shorts and white T-shirt, arms flailing about, parading around the kitchen table singing: 'Do Do Do, The Chocolate Rumba.'

He was impressively in key.

Max and Charlie were squirming with glee as they followed him, jumping up and down, attempting to grab hold and cling on to his T-shirt with their chubby little hands. The three of them formed a bright caterpillar of colour, as they marched, giggling back and forth, Paul in his underwear, the boys dressed in their flannelette yellow and red pyjamas splattered with navy blue teddy bears.

'Do Do Do, The Chocolate Rumba.'

It was enchanting to watch, this man, my husband, with these two little people, wrapped in magic, totally captured by his charm.

They all sang, Paul clutching two plastic beakers of hot chocolate he'd been heating up for the boys in the microwave. The tops were firmly sealed as he vigorously shook them about, one in each hand like maracas.

I was both crying and laughing. As I gazed at my family, undiscovered in their joy, I thought that this is happiness. A blissful fragment of time, seized in a brief moment. Whatever happiness may be, I do know that what I saw is pure, unconditional love.

One morning shortly after I had dropped both boys at their classrooms, I bumped into Sheila Abbott in the corridor. My heart sank as she beckoned me into her office. I still had not overcome the inexplicable feelings of fear and inadequacy I was always reduced to in her company. Her formidable manner evoked childhood memories of my own school days. I'd like to think I no longer quake in my shoes when faced with institutional authority, but some habits are hard to shake off. In typical Sheila-like fashion she came right to the point. With her own contempt clearly visible, she explained that one of the parents in Max's class had attempted to gather support for a formal objection to Max's presence in the school. It would appear that these parents, along with some others, were concerned that their children's education was suffering because of Max being in the class.

To this day such an argument confuses me. Max had a full-time support worker, Jackie, who was encouraged to allow him the freedom to develop many skills unaided. This in turn would then naturally free up Jackie, who, whilst keeping an eagle eye on Max, would help other students. This arrangement could only be a positive asset in an already large class. A petition was mentioned, but I don't think any such action got under way. As soon as Sheila caught the mood of these parents, she had hauled them into her office to make her own feelings known. Sheila relayed to me how she politely informed these parents of all the benefits Max's involvement with the class brought and that she could genuinely see no valid reason why Max's presence could be considered as detrimental. She also suggested that, if the parents were unhappy with the situation, instead of whipping up unpleasant feelings in her school, they should take steps to search for a replacement school for their child.

Despite having the unquestioning support of Sheila Abbott and all her staff, the incident left Paul and me shell-shocked. We found ourselves questioning the opinions of all the parents whose children mixed with Max, and began to feel very suspicious towards everyone. We felt isolated, but we were determined to grasp hold of the amazing support and strength all the Brooklands staff showed us. Still we couldn't escape the feeling that while people thought that inclusion was a good idea, it was a far better idea if it happened in somebody else's backyard.

By now I'd recognised that our lives did follow a pattern except that it wasn't a predictable one. There would always be ups and downs and as much as we tried to enjoy the ups, I now think we could have done better. At the same time there was no telling when we'd find ourselves in a potentially calamitous situation with Max's health. An innocent cold could lead to a chest infection that could then lead to hospital. Something that was so humdrum for a normal family became a big deal in ours, often involving frantic dashes to doctors and pharmacies.

Max had regular visits to the Brompton Hospital to monitor the hole in his heart. The appointment was always an ordeal, a kind of stress test on our own hearts really. It would generally last just over an hour and during that time I was so tense I'd forget to breathe. I would have to remind myself to inhale deeply as I sat and waited for the verdict on Max's health. Any news that was delivered should not have been a surprise, since we had a fair idea of what was going on. Nonetheless it was an almighty shock when the cardiologist suggested that Max have a heart operation. This was to be an exploratory procedure, a catheterisation, not to close the hole, but to get a better idea of any damage that it may be causing to his lungs. It would also provide essential details on the condition of the hole and whether leaving the closure operation to a later date was still an option. I think what surprised me most about it all was Paul's reaction. When we got back to the car he just wasn't the Paul I knew.

'I just can't do this,' he said. 'I can't go through with it, I'm not strong enough, I can't do it.'

At that moment, I could see it was more a cry for help than a factual statement. And for a rare moment all thoughts of my son were pushed to one side as I saw my husband battle with our worrying news. He looked like a wounded animal and watching him struggle with the idea of Max having an operation felt like having my heart pierced. My natural tendency towards pragmatism took over and I told him that he may not have much choice in the matter. That makes me sound like I was stronger than I was. In truth, I felt sick to the pit of my stomach. The journey back home was a long, silent one with both Paul and me marooned in our thoughts. Max was only six years old and those hideous visions of tiny white coffins came into my brain once more. Oblivious to the despair we were feeling, Max happily gazed out of the car window checking out the big red London buses. He loved to spot the gigantic posters displaying the forthcoming movies he had such a passion for.

We decided to seek a second opinion and took Max to a cardiologist at Great Ormond Street Hospital who wholeheartedly agreed with the recommendations of the experts at the Brompton. I don't know whether we were expecting them to quell our anxiety but the visit actually exacerbated it. There was no turning back now. The procedure was absolutely necessary. The only control we now had was over the speed in which the procedure was performed. The days leading up to the operation were agonising. Once again, Max had a slight cold and the operation hung in the balance. Scared and uncertain, we arrived at the Brompton Hospital very early one cold November morning in order for Max to be prepped for the procedure. We had purposely kept our explanation of the visit to Max to the bare minimum. The plan was to explain things and support Max's understanding as he went along. I have to say the staff were simply wonderful. They treated Max with kindness and respect and did all they could to make the visit as pleasant as possible.

The children's ward of the Brompton Hospital is a brightly coloured, welcoming place, but it is also a grim and humbling microcosm of reality. Row upon row of giant beds are filled with tiny little child-sized bumps. Each one has their own heart-breaking story involving pain and trauma and many are facing an uncertain future. Even in such bleak and sad circumstances, they all still manage to radiate light, as children seem to do. Some have no hair, others are so pale and weak you feel them literally slipping away before your very eyes. There are a lot of tears – brave tears – but tears all the same. It's a place you'd never choose to take your child, yet it is full of kindness, respect and optimism. The amazing staff must feel at times that they have nothing left to give as they witness unfair and cruel blows of fate. But there are many children who walk out of such a place better and stronger because of it. They have been granted the gift of seeing tomorrow, which hardly makes them lucky but, under the circumstances, it's the best they could wish for.

And there you are, waiting in line, wondering if you are going to be one of the parents of the 'lucky' ones. And with the waiting come the inevitable dark thoughts: please let it be our son that wins this one, choose him, please. Meanwhile you have to make sure you behave in a cheery manner, because you are surrounded by little people. You masterfully adopt a facade of complete denial and insincere joviality.

In terms of our own son we were fortunate that his age and his DS gave us a degree of control, so he was not fully aware of what was to come or the possible consequences of the procedure. He was assigned a nurse to walk with us through everything, every single blood test and X-ray. What touched us most was her genuine concern for Max's welfare. They even suggested that we take Max home with us on the night before his operation, once all the tests were complete, because we lived relatively close to the hospital and they thought Max would do better at home. He was to return early the next morning. This seemed a far better idea than having him fretting in a strange hospital bed. We gladly accepted the suggestion and arrived home relatively late that night, but very grateful to be there.

As I've said previously, one certainty about our life

was that it was unpredictable. In what can only be described as a random occurrence, Max managed to have an accident that would almost jeopardise his operation the next day. We had put him to bed with a sigh of momentary relief and quickly retired to bed ourselves. We hadn't been in bed long when we heard a loud thump. I dashed in to Max's room to find him face down on the floor in a pool of blood. He was completely motionless and for a split second I feared he was dead. Overcome by panic, I pulled him into my arms screaming at him to wake up. He awoke but was very groggy. I had no idea if this was because he had fallen into a deep sleep, or if he was injured in some way. After what seemed like for ever, Max surfaced from his dreams and belted out a welcome cry, if only to reassure us that he was fully conscious and still very much alive. The memory of that moment still makes my stomach flip. We will never be entirely sure what happened but it seems Max had fallen through a small gap between the top bars of his bunk bed and smashed on to the floor below. From that day onwards he has never slept in a bunk bed but I still cannot entirely fathom how it happened. That this incident came out of nowhere was a poignant reminder that however hard we tried, we would never be in control.

The next morning we arrived at the Brompton

Hospital feeling like the worst parents to walk the earth. As the anaesthetist examined Max, we explained to him what had happened. Not surprisingly we were very nervous that Max would no longer be fit for surgery. He had a large red mark across his face where he had hit the carpet and I was convinced that he would be sent home and we would have to go through all this agony again. Part of me would have welcomed this, but a larger part of me wanted to get it over with. In the event, the anaesthetist gave him the all clear and we were ready to go ahead. The actual procedure was quite impressive. A small tube would be inserted into a vein in Max's thigh and gently coaxed up through his body to his heart. Once in the correct place, various tests could be carried out to see the extent of Max's condition. Ultimately the results would determine whether we could continue to delay any invasive surgery – giving his body the chance to repair the hole itself – or if it was time to call a halt and proceed with open-heart surgery. After watching Max go under, we kissed him goodbye and watched them wheel him away. Paul and I must have looked like two abandoned sheep. We just stood there clinging to one another, unable to focus on what to do or where to go. Eventually we arrived in the hospital café. A cup of tea sat in front of me getting colder as I cried. The tears would not stop coming and

I'm not sure I wanted them to. After a few hours we decided to make our way back to the ward, wondering why we had not yet been called to Max's side. In the lift on the way up we met a doctor who had been assisting our own cardiologist. I remembered her because when I had seen her earlier, I wondered about how hot she must have felt in a full burka in operating gear under hospital lights. She smiled at us and told us things went well. Were we safe? I kept my reserve but I allowed myself the positive thought that my cherished child would not have to be sliced open.

Eventually Max was wheeled back into his room. We were reassured that he had successfully come out of the anaesthetic, but he was still heavily asleep. His nurse clucked over him like a mother hen, regularly checking his leg where they had entered the catheter and busying herself with paperwork at his side. She tried to coax us into stepping out for a coffee, but we were unable to leave our son. We planted ourselves on either side of him, holding on to his little hands, gazing at him, smelling him and watching his chest rise and fall with every breath. There was a funny moment when he eventually woke up. Croissants are a favourite food of Max's which we rarely allow him and we'd placed one on his chest as our 'sorry' gift. It may not have been much, but when he saw the plump, flaky crescent resting on his chest Max rolled his eyes and gave us the most wonderful smile.

We had another long wait for the cardiologist to finish his entire surgery list before he emerged to pass on his findings. Despite his huge responsibilities, he was a calm, thoughtful man with no apparent vanity. Dealing with the future of young children and coping with their overwrought and anxious parents cannot be easy.

He spoke to us with great tact and was careful not to make any false promises or inflict any unnecessary fear. It almost felt like we were joining him in the decision process. He informed us that Max's lungs were experiencing no significant damage and that all the readings were within the normal limits. For now he felt that Max could be given some more time in which his body might repair the hole itself. It was a grey area, a decision he did not make lightly and he stressed that he would be happy to be guided by us if we wanted the hole closed. To put Max through an unnecessary traumatic operation would have been a dreadfully selfish act in my opinion. I could never have forgiven myself if I had grown impatient, found I could no longer tolerate the unknown and demanded an operation, only for there to have been some dreadful consequence. No, I would be patient and not place my son in that precarious position. The hole in his heart is a constant threat to his health and a massive black cloud that always hovers over us. But then both Paul and I felt we needed to wait. We were relieved that the grace of a bit more time had been granted to us and we looked forward to taking our son home.

Chapter Thirteen

24 August

Max has been at St Mary's summer scheme again. He went last year and, against all odds, won, yes, WON, the 'Pop Idol' competition they hold at the end of every week. The carer who was with him assured me that he really did win fair and square in a democratic vote, and that frankly he deserved to.

This year he'd raised his game and gone for a full rendition of 'It's Not Unusual' by Tom Jones. I've watched him practise, and I have to admit he's good. Nice touch at the end when he strips off his denim shirt and flings it, in a most provocative way, into the audience. Paul and I gently suggested to him that this year he might not win. Obviously we think he's fantastic and should be a winner every year, but invariably life just does not pan out that way. We suggested he needed to consider that he

*might not take home the crowning glory of tiara
and sash, which he received last year.*

*I must admit I was rather nervous during the
afternoon, and positively neurotic waiting for Paul
to pick him up and bring him home. He came
through the door grinning from ear to ear.*

*'I won Mum!' he gleefully announced. I glanced
at Paul in total disbelief, but no, Paul confirmed
with a proud nod, that indeed our Max had once
again surprised us, and seized the moment for
himself. Unbelievable.*

A few years after Max was born, somebody – and I
wish I could remember who – suggested that I put
his name down at Chickenshed. I knew nothing about the
organisation, only that it was an inclusive company
inspired and run by two dynamic women. They had a
reputation of running an impressive, talented theatre
group that reflected their own strong motivation and
ethics and they achieved some magical results with children with special needs, including children with DS. I was
still on my manic quest, feeling that I needed to cover
every eventuality for my son and so, without paying too
much attention, I requested an application form. I
returned it duly completed, noting that the waiting list
was years, not months, and forgot all about it.

When Max was seven we received a letter inviting him to join Chickenshed. By this time I had gathered more details about the company, and had learned about their important, sometimes life-changing, work over the past 30 years. I was so delighted that Max was going to be given the opportunity to be part of it. He was welcomed into the nurturing environment of the Chickenshed workshops and took to the experience with such glee and intense commitment that it would prove to be one of the most important partnerships in his life to date. In the six years he has been living and breathing the theatre, it has unquestionably been a major lifeline socially, emotionally and creatively.

Part of the magic is the independence they encourage. When Paul took Max to his first workshop, he was momentarily taken aback. There was no suggestion that he would stay with Max on the visit. In fact, he was told the pick-up time, politely invited to leave Max with them and forced to watch his son happily trot into the theatre holding Charlotte Bull's hand – the Children's Theatre Director – as she introduced him to everyone. Paul was rather put out and felt compelled to hang about in the bar, just in case he was needed. We had never experienced Max being asked to survive on his own, with just the surrounding community to provide support. Until that moment he'd always had a specified carer in whatever activity he happened to be doing. Here we were being asked – no, told – to leave Max's many needs to the supervisors and his new family of co-performers. This was a very difficult concept for Paul and me to accept. Unable to cope with his discomfort on his own, Paul rang me at home.

'I wasn't allowed to stay.'

'What! You're joking.'

'They wanted him to go in on his own. I wasn't given the option of staying.'

'Oh my God, how long till he comes out?'

'Another hour.'

'Do they know where you are?'

'No, not really, I'm staying in the bar though, I might get a chance to peek into the theatre and check that he's okay.'

'Ring me when you pick him up.'

'Okay.'

An hour later, a beaming Max ran into Paul's arms declaring he'd had the best time ever. From that moment on he's always gone on his own. It's the only place he's really been able to behave at his appropriate age level, because that's what's expected from him. When he does need help, it's there for him, given by the Chickenshed community with kindness and respect. There have been times when he's struggled with things like getting to the toilet, changing his pull-ups, soiling himself through nerves and not being able to communicate a problem he may have. But not only has he survived, he's thrived. He loves it. Chickenshed have an instinctive understanding of people with a disability and they don't wallow in the obvious. There are some with profound disabilities who attend the workshops – and the supervisors strive in order to work around such obstacles, exploring different avenues and incorporating alternatives. Mary Ward and Jo Collins, the two women who founded Chickenshed some 30 years ago, possess enormous vision. Their simple, uncluttered concept was of a place where all people could feel a sense of acceptance and belonging. They have taken what self-belief each child has and directed it into something special and remarkable.

I defy anyone to experience a performance at Chickenshed and not force back prickly tears. These aren't tears of pity, but an acknowledgement of the extraordinary determination and unity that always emanates from the stage. Chickenshed doesn't patronise its students, or indulge them with kindness. They are a formidable theatre company who expect the highest standard and commitment from all their members. That's what makes it so special; you can see that determination in all the students, whatever their shape, size or ability. The participants give their utmost, willingly and enthusiastically, because what they get back is very special indeed. They develop a sense of worth and inclusion.

For Max this experience was akin to a homecoming. He soon slotted comfortably into the ethos of Chickenshed and began to grow and develop as a rich and thoughtful performer. In this safe place, Max has explored his own sensitivity and compelling need to express himself. He has reaped the rewards from performances that produce emotional highs for him like nothing else. Chickenshed has also been a welcome respite for Max from the struggle with his everyday life. Instead of being a round peg, squashed into a square hole, it's given him a freedom to explore, with relish, the excitement of his imagination and the interaction with like-minded individuals who share his need to perform.

And boy, does he adore the place. It is the backbone of his life and is irreplaceable. We could never think of moving to an area that robbed him of his access to Chickenshed. To watch him while he is performing, either at the workshops, or during a show, is such a treat. A deep glow comes from within him and he radiates an enviable happiness. It's intoxicating to watch. How I wish I had something in my life that fuels me with such passion! Max has been a biker, a mouse and a punk fairy, and he's had the chance to take a central role in a performance. He devours whatever is thrown at him. Of course there are egos: by their very nature, entertainers and performers must have egos to be able to go on to a stage and hold the audience's attention, but it's all held together with respect and modesty.

One evening after a performance of 'The Nutcracker and the Mouse King' where Max was playing a mouse, Paul had come to pick up Max. They were both making their way towards the front doors when they bumped into Mary Ward, one of the co-founders, who said some special and very complimentary things about Max. She spoke about him having a true talent for acting, saying she had noticed that he liked to 'push the boundaries', a noticeable sign of a natural. She felt that he had real potential and mentioned how much she enjoyed working with him. Paul was so proud.

Not only was Chickenshed a place of spiritual refuge for Max, it also gave him the chance to develop the skills for his break into film and television. Through years of regular involvement in the theatre Max proved to everyone and particularly himself that he was a very competent actor. When a casting agent was calling around looking for a capable young actor to play the part of Ben in the film *Notes on a Scandal*, Max's name quickly came to mind with a number of people she spoke to.

But Chickenshed will always keep him grounded. Whilst he has dipped his toe into other projects with considerable celebrity status, this year, for the Chickenshed production of *Grimm Nights and Ever After Days*, Max played a tree! He was decked out in full army combat uniform, including boots and braces, and had to look rough, rural, and rustic. And he *loved* every minute of it.

Chapter Fourteen

9 March

I have slipped into a really unhealthy habit that has to stop. On my way up to bed, I always stop by to kiss my sleeping angels. It's probably the most delicious time of the day. They are tucked up safe and sound, asleep in their beds. I can just enjoy their sheer beauty without them shattering the illusion with any backchat. Charlie always stirs ever so slightly, after I've planted an irresistible kiss on his cheek and usually mutters something about loving me. Max is always flat out and never moves. Paul will come along later to lift him to the toilet. He flatly refuses me, and he's a big chap, so it's a no-brainer to leave him for Paul.

For the last few days, every night, on my way up to bed, I've perched at the bottom of Max's bed and just wept, sad, sorry tears of grief and anger. We live on the continual precipice of disaster: well, that's how it feels to me. No sooner have we wrapped up some calamity and put it behind us, than another rears its ugly head. I am constantly on alert, sometimes having to remind myself to breathe. Max has so much going on inside him, that never even reaches the surface. It breaks my heart: he must feel so lonely, so desperate to get someone to listen, but he can't cut through that film of silence.

I must stop this habit, it is self destructive as well as maudlin and unhealthy, but I just can't seem to.

Having Max in our lives and coping with his daily needs has been a life-changing, positive experience. We will never know a different life. On the other hand, there are times I would give anything for him not to have Down's syndrome, just to see how I think my son could have been. Yet while l brood and ponder, Paul will do no such thing. Paul views Max's condition in a very different light to me. He feels Max is who he is *because* of his DS: it is a fundamental part of what makes him Max.

While I am always looking over my shoulder, bracing myself for what may be coming, I am learning to enjoy Max in the moment. He is a funny, charming, outrageously cheeky individual, who has the capacity to brighten the dullest day and remind you to look for the sunshine in life. He can be frustratingly stubborn and hates any kind of change, but if things are working for him then he's an utter delight to be around. He likes to be busy all the time and adores social events such as his dance class or Chickenshed. He is passionate about film and theatre and will watch movies again and again. He is forever putting on 'shows' around the house and demands an audience. He's bright and enthusiastic but at the same time he's easily knocked off his perch. He is also very aware he has DS.

Being with him quickly eradicates any superficial, phoney aspirations you may harbour. You find yourself becoming intolerant of a society that must have a particular 'in vogue' fashion accessory in order to be seen as worthwhile. With Max you don't waste your life thinking about being cool, glossy or successful: you just get on with it.

For me, the change from a little boy who could just about fit within the broad parameters of infants, to a young boy clearly not fitting in with his peers, arrived when Max started the junior school at Brooklands. Now it was time to leave behind the nurturing teachers like Jaia, Mike and Carole and the caring classroom assistants like Wendy, Adrienne and Jan. I no longer had the certainty of knowing that all of these lovely people would be there for Max. The junior school of

Brooklands was a very good school, but was run by an entirely different team. It also catered to older, very able children. Max and his accompanying baggage could no longer be hidden in the classroom so easily. By this time he had developed a strong stubborn streak, which made him a bit of an enemy unto himself. His carer, Jackie, made the move to the juniors with him, and she was fantastic.

However, as time went on she found it necessary to remove him from the general class and give him individual tuition – in the corridor. Her professionalism was outstanding, but not far into the academic year we could see the gap between Max and his peers widening. Whilst he was a very popular child who seemed to bring out the best in his fellow classmates, it was painfully apparent that they were also just being kind to him, tolerating him even. This would happen to the point where they'd let him behave in a way that would not be considered acceptable by another child. He had one or two little friends like Louis and the twins, Pip and Tog, who he would probably consider his good mates. And they were, but only just. There were many other children who were friendly to him too, in the sense that they would be happy to pair up with him on an activity or wave hello in the morning. However, there was always a limit of tolerance and interest, which meant they wouldn't particularly consider themselves to be real mates with him. At the end of the day, he wasn't likely to be invited around for tea after school.

There were also many parents who were genuinely welcoming of Max into the school and supportive of me and Paul. One of the benefits of Max attending Brooklands is that I met an amazing lady who has since become a treasured friend. Caroline is the kind of individual you might meet just once in your lifetime. They say opposites attract, but Caroline and I are almost identical. Not only do we share the same star sign, our birthdays being one day apart, but we are the same age, albeit exactly a year apart. We even look alike.

We had no obvious connection within the school, our children never shared the same class, but something brought us together. Years later I can only feel truly blessed. Soon after we first met, we committed to walking every Wednesday. We'd go to Hampstead Heath and walk for an hour or so and then enjoy a much-needed cup of tea in Kenwood House. During our walk we'd discuss things – everything, really – and always manage to put the world to rights. There are so many ways in which Caroline is a kindred spirit but I feel there is one in which she is particularly close to me. Although the circumstances are entirely different, Caroline also battles with profound grief. Five years ago she lost her mother to cancer and it still feels like yesterday to her. The strength she has demonstrated in coping with such a cruel and devastating loss has in turn helped me. We joke that Caroline's mum watches over us as we walk every week. She certainly holds the rain at bay: we arrive in the pouring rain and it stops long enough for us to walk, talk and drink tea. We drive out from the car park and the rain starts again. Uncanny, but true. On every walk, we find ourselves sharing our grief but we also have a lot of laughs. Invariably we leave each other with our confidence boosted, and with a respect and love for one another that you just can't define.

Without Max's vibrant character, perhaps his increasing isolation at Brooklands wouldn't have mattered as much as it did. But I could see Max becoming more and more alienated from his classmates and more importantly, I could see his perception of this. By his very nature he wanted to be in there, in the thick of it, laughing and joking with his friends. He needs to command an audience and be the centre of attention, yet he was reduced to being an outsider, and he knew it. He became very mildly depressed and I knew it was time to do something about it. It took a great deal of strength, but I forced myself to go and visit some special needs schools in the local area. I was actually very relieved and impressed with what I saw. Special schools can be scary places. They are full of children like Max, people who don't fit into society for one reason or another.

The first rather striking fact that greets you when you are shown around these places is that the majority of pupils are boys. Only one in ten children at a special needs school is a girl. I have no idea why this is, but it certainly has a practical impact on the gender balance. While I will admit I found these places intimidating and had not really envisaged placing any child of mine there, I did sense an atmosphere of calm acceptance. So much so, that when I visited a junior school called Northway and was warmly welcomed by its impressive and committed head teacher, Lesley Burgess, I knew this was a good place. It was somewhere that Max could be himself and also have the opportunity to thrive. Make no mistake, Max is a vibrant individual capable of excelling at many things. His ability to act and perform had already proved that. Apparently I didn't stand a chance of getting him in. No place. No funding. Not a hope in hell.

Now I'm the type of person whose vocabulary does not include 'no'. So I don't like having it said to me and can even lose sight of what the *no* was for. To be told that Max had *no* chance of attending Northway was all the provocation I required. I had decided Max would be happy in this school. The professionals advising us agreed and in my mind that was where he should go.

In the event we had no trouble getting Max into Northway and this may have been an accumulation of many things. I think our message of no tolerance to the bullying tactics of the local education authority must have played an important part in the process. Perhaps it was because his file is so ridiculously thick, and that our attitude from the start was one of very polite, but unyielding commitment? Ultimately there was no real argument to prevent Max from moving schools, and I suspect the local educational authority had no wish to provoke us into taking any further action against them.

The most delightful thing about the move to Northway was Max; he was so up for it, so excited by the prospect of not being at the very bottom of the ocean. For a long time at Brooklands he had felt that he would always be at the bottom and that it was pointless trying to compete with anyone. By not attempting anything in the first place he found a way to suppress his disappointment. That's not to say he didn't have an inkling that he could do more: he saw what he could achieve at Chickenshed, and he also attended the weekly dance class for people with DS where he felt very relaxed and was accepted for who he was. His dance class, like Chickenshed, is a much-cherished part of his life.

It was a sad day when Max finally left Brooklands, but a part of me felt tremendous relief. I would no longer have to fake it. I could just allow Max to be Max, and not continually have to strive for him to conform. It was extremely hard to say goodbye to his carer Jackie, who by now had been with him for many years, but I knew it was the right thing to do. From the day Max started at Northway, he became a different child. They were very pleased with his learning ability and astonished at how well he settled in and the progress he made.

Initially we had hoped that Max would spend at least two years at this school. When he arrived he entered his age-appropriate year, automatically jumping across the two years he had been delayed at Brooklands. We thought he could do year six twice, and gain full benefit from the school. However, it soon became clear that there was no way Max could stay there past year six. He was doing too well and so would have to follow his peers to secondary school.

Ironically the only area where the school had any concerns was with Max's social skills! That was the very reason why we had sent him to mainstream school in the first place! It would seem that Max had never been given the opportunity of developing natural social skills. He had always been babysat and cosseted and therefore missed out on the normal rough and tumble of the play-ground, and the skills that children develop through such interaction. A great deal of effort was now made for Max to learn social skills in his new environment, including involving him in individual social-skill work-shops. Whilst he made up for lost time, I often wonder if the attention he received earlier on is responsible – in part – for his diva-like attitude to the world.

I still feel Max could have benefited from staying on at Northway for two years, but after one year, he made the transition to the local special needs secondary school, Oak Lodge. I had visited this school a few years previously, when I had first begun to question Max's future in mainstream school. Sadly there is no perfect option in our present education system for a child with DS. Obviously I can only speak from what little experi-ence I have, and each child is undoubtedly very different. But it is clear to me that there is no ideal place to send children with DS; in my mind they can slip between two worlds. The world of mainstream educa-tion, which although it reflects real life, is fast and sophisticated and too competitive, and the world of special needs, which is a completely different environ-ment: non-competitive, operating at a relaxed pace and safe, but perhaps pupils are not exposed to a more real-istic take on life. A unit just for people with DS attached to a mainstream school with, most importantly, a bucketful of money, would perhaps be the best option. This would provide them with a safe environment where they could be educated on a level footing with like-minded students, but get the beneficial exposure of real life. As far as I'm aware nothing like this exists.

Oak Lodge soon picked up on a major gap in Max's learning. They quickly established that Max had tricked us all. He was 11, yet had the reading age far below that of a six-year-old. Whilst there are no set parameters for children with DS and their capacity to read, Max was fooling us into thinking he had a reading age far older than was actually the case. He had learnt all the books in his reading system – The Oxford Reading Tree – by heart. This system is used by both Brooklands and Northway, and is, quite rightly, heralded as an excellent reading system. Max could read beautifully from all the books in the series, and convincingly lead anyone into thinking that he could read properly. Not so. It was only when his teacher thought something wasn't quite right and dug below his surface skills that she realised Max was actually unable to identify all the letters from the alphabet. Although I thought I had procured every necessary tool for my son, at the age of 11 he was illiterate.

Paul and I were devastated, angry and racked with

tremendous guilt. We went to great lengths to have him assessed. We checked for dyslexia or any clue to this massive discrepancy. We found nothing. For some reason he had managed to slip through the net. All his peers from his dance class could read and write to varying degrees. Max is just as intelligent as his friends, so where had it gone wrong? I have an overwhelming sense that I have failed him, that I've let him down and deprived him of a basic skill for life, one that he is actually capable of achieving. People tell me that I cannot look back and chastise myself for decisions I took in the past in good faith. I know they're right, but it's still distressing.

Julia Sherrard is a private child development adviser who came highly recommended. Although she isn't a specialist in children with Down's syndrome, she is very experienced with all sorts of children. I contacted Julia and explained about Max. At 12 he was a much older child than those Julia usually worked with, but she was very happy to take him on and give it a try. Secretly, I think she welcomed the challenge. I now take Max out of school to visit Julia twice a week. She's fantastic, doggedly persistent, and determined to get our son to read. Max loves going. I suspect the main attraction is Julia's adorable Wheaten Terrier, Cookie. Cookie never barks at Max, but whoops with delight at him, most probably because Max is permitted to feed treats to Cookie when Julia feels he has done well.

The road to Max achieving any degree of literacy is going to be a very long one. He has been going to Julia's for an hour twice a week for just over a year now, and he has made some progress. In fact, we are delighted with him. Both Julia and I feel there are clear indications that he has the capacity to learn. At the same time it's painfully slow. He is also his own worst enemy. Whilst he's with Julia, he is cooperative and will finish tasks she sets for him. Once he gets home, it's a different story. His stubbornness, fear of failure, and teenage hormones blight his learning. Having said all that we're immensely proud of him; he desperately wants to read and write (if only to make sure he never misses his favourite programmes on the telly!) and must feel so frustrated and angry, especially when he sees his brother happily devouring books and writing stunning poetry.

Oak Lodge is a fantastic school with committed staff, but there is one major problem. Special schools are unable to specialise. An alarming lack of funding, politics and bureaucracy of this crazy world prevent any specialist school from being *special*. I find it wholly inappropriate that children of very different and complex needs are grouped together and that teachers and support staff are expected to educate and develop these individuals to their full capacity. The structure and ethos of Oak Lodge, and many of the systems and programs they implement, are amazing and should be applauded. But the task that lies ahead of the gifted, dedicated staff every new academic year is daunting.

Sometimes I think I'm seeing something so painfully obvious, something that is simply basic common sense. Am I the only one screaming in frustration? The result of this inability to specialise is that my son who has a genetic condition has previously been forced to sit next to a violent, disturbed individual. Both need care, but that care is necessarily very different.

On balance, special school is the more appropriate option for Max. It affords him the right to be accepted for who he is on his own terms. He has friends who are his good mates; they do not just tolerate him or show kindness towards him. They are his equals. Yes, they are different and unable to sustain friendships in quite the same way you or I would choose, but they are genuine friends. The curriculum is definitely more appropriate too. They learn life skills: how to cook, how to read a tube map and generally how to exist in this noisy, busy world. The fact that they don't tackle logarithms, or algebra, is not too much of an issue in the grander scheme of things. What is most important is that Max is happy. That's what we have always measured everything by. It's not hard to spot, but fundamentally it is the most important aspect of his life. And ours.

Chapter Fifteen

11 June

Max pulled a corker the other day. He does this with relentless ease and I am very near to tearing my hair out in clumps. He was playing up in his room and I foolishly was led into a false sense of security. I assumed he was up there playing with his toys and watching a movie. He had been contentedly doing this when I had passed his door earlier. How naive am I? I can't believe that I still allow myself to indulge in the fantasy that Max can be left more than a half an hour by himself.

It was some time later that I made the ascent up to his room to give him a bottle of mineral water to drink before he got his supper. I entered his room after my polite knock on the door. Max was sat with the face of an angel, only that face was covered in blue play-dough. When is he going to grow out of eating this stuff? He's 12! He was very aware that he was in big, big trouble. I asked him if he'd been eating play-dough and for a split second the lie could be detected as clear as day right across his face. He denied it emphatically, wrongly assuming that because he had eaten all the evidence he'd got away with it.

An old box of play-dough with little plastic moulds to make flowers and crazy snails was lying on the bed. I recognised it from the bundle of fun things Mum and Dad gave Max for Christmas last year. Still, he continued with the lie and I had to speedily think on my toes. I decided to use the crafty punishment I had recently discovered. I banned him from any bread for the whole of the next day. Clever: by withholding his most treasured food it hurts, if only a little. By way of perfect reinforcement, the next day meant Max had the agony of sitting through a family barbeque without a bun for his burger. Later at tea, he was forced to watch his brother and a friend happily chomp on freshly baked ciabatta rolls stuffed with tuna and mayonnaise. When I gave him his tomato soup he shot me such a look of disdain I swear he would have thrown his supper at me given half a chance.

Over the years Paul and I have been forced to battle with never-ending obstacles in our desire to get the very best for Max. Sometimes the barriers are the very people who are supposed to be helping. I have often felt it would be nice if, just occasionally, we had a warrior – a superhero – in our corner to help us fight our battles. But we don't. While our experiences have made us somewhat cynical and suspicious, we've also gained a great deal of insight and understanding into how various systems work. It saddens us that money is at the centre of it all.

In Max's statement of educational needs it clearly said that speech therapy was a fundamental necessity of his development. Because it was entered into the appropriate section of his statement of special needs, it legally had to be provided. Sadly it was no surprise when our local educational authority failed to do this. This system failed many children; Max was just one of them. There are many situations in this life where you need to shout and those of us who shout the loudest and keep it up are the ones who will eventually get some redress. Thus, Paul and I have learnt to shout very loud and not to give up, although we have sometimes wished we could. It would be both a relief and a welcome luxury to be able to roll over instead of being cast as troublemakers, the irritating people who insist on making an almighty fuss. Without each other to rely on for valuable support and encouragement, I wonder if we would have been able to stay resolute and determined when those in authority were clamping their hands firmly over their ears and wishing that we would disappear. I often think of parents and carers who are not as fortunate as Paul and I, who do not have the unity that we cherish and must stand alone and shout. Perhaps the local educational authority banks on them eventually losing their voice and giving up?

As a parent trawling through the education system, it seems to me that politicians and bureaucrats are a very long way from the front line when it comes to the war on special needs. I say 'war', because that's what it feels like. They create glossy, idealistic policies and procedures, which filter down though an inadequate system. The whole thing is a disaster. Although Max had a statement of educational needs, we had to fight tooth and nail to achieve even that much. And then, when we were able to hold it in our sweaty paws, it was hardly worth the paper it was written on. Most of the contents became a remote dream, provisions that would be wonderful but were not in any way viable or possible in the current set-up. If it were not so grim and dire and did not involve such vulnerable and fragile young people, it would be laughable.

Our latest battle involved Max not getting any speech therapy, a clear violation of his statement. Week after week, term after term, the local educational authority let him down. Meanwhile, Paul and I were paying privately for speech therapy. It was a chronic matter, one which had been festering and rotting for some years. We felt Max couldn't wait for an angel to appear and wave her magic wand, nor could he afford to lose out in such a valuable area of his development. It was vital that he be given the chance to develop his speech to the highest potential. As an adult, Max wouldn't stand a chance in society without adequate speech. As a child, people were generous in their tolerance of him. Later, that tolerance would wane. Max would know it and have yet another reason to sink into despair.

When I think about how we had to beg and scream for such a fundamental right, a deep rage begins to course though me. This issue just kept building and so did both our determination and our anger. We took the local educational authority on, and ended up in tribunal. We won, but it cost us thousands.

We wisely sought the services of Jack Rabinowicz, a lawyer specialising in education. He came highly recommended, was focused, smart and just what we needed. Without him we would have struggled, but having his expertise allowed us to clearly show the education authority's true colours. It was so obvious that Max required the speech therapy we were asking for. Max and Charlie were only eight and six at the time, so they were completely unaware of the build-up to the day of the tribunal, but the atmosphere in our home at the time was tense and stressed. I remember taking a photograph of Max to show the panel, just to show them the boy all the stacks of papers and reports were referring to; I wanted to bring Max to life. When we won we were delighted with the result, but a strong residual anger lingered as we questioned why we had to go to such lengths.

Should we have ignored the fight, taken the money that we used for our legal expenses and poured it all into giving Max as much speech therapy as he could tolerate? It's a question I often tussle with but it would have meant giving in to a bully. Is it better to work with what the system gives you in order for a smoother path or take a principled stand against the bullies? I still don't really know. No doubt there are arguments for both sides and I will say it was a hard road to travel down. I'm still not sure if there were any winners. One vital thing that emerged from all our battles is that our local educational authority knows we are fighters. They now know that when we ask for something Max is entitled to, we will not stop until he gets it. Has this made our path smoother? I'm not sure, but part of me feels proud that we did fight for our son, and that we didn't shy away from sticking up for him, right through to the bitter end.

When you have a child with special needs there is little respite from bureaucracy. Another source of horror and frustration was the application form for disability living allowance. This is a benefit (the classification 'benefit' I find quite ironic) granted to an individual with moderate to severe learning or physical disabilities. I understand that rigorous checks must be made on any applicant's entitlement. I'm sure the abuse of benefits is rife. But even so, for the thousands of perfectly eligible people, the process you must go through is degrading and shameful. The actual application forms require a good healthy tree of paper; the questions are repetitive and meticulously intricate, and must be difficult for many people to comprehend, let alone answer properly. It just seems unfair that people who are already going through so much stress are forced to endure even more. Putting aside all the arguments for such thorough questioning, the real disgust I have with the form lies in one of the final sections. The instructions for this section state that it must be completed by a 'friend or neighbour'. Such a task would suggest that regardless of what painful details you provide, the answers can not be believed. The remarks of a third party seem more important. It would seem that, on these intensely personal matters, the authorities give more credibility to your neighbour than to yourself.

As you might gather, being a person with special needs or looking after a person with special needs can be a very isolating existence. Some levels of personal maintenance and individual requirements are deeply private and personal. Being forced to find someone to back up your application means having to divulge intimate details to someone who really doesn't need to know them. The trauma and embarrassment of confessing to a friend that you are actually applying for such a benefit, and then having to ask them to write a page about how they see the disability in question is not only plain stupid, but totally unnecessary and degrading. There is nothing right about this process. It sickens me that the authorities can't figure out a system which is just as competent and accurate, but also sensitive and respectful. I do not want to involve friends or neighbours in my personal finances or requests for care benefit. I cannot see why it is required since every professional involved with Max was required to be listed. Details of their latest reports are made readily available and even his teachers were asked to comment on his condition.

When I first got the forms for Max, I gasped with shock. My day was already packed to the brim, so I decided to tackle it bit by bit. I pledged to finish two pages of the application form every day. I figured if I managed to keep to my word, it would take me about six weeks to complete. Having to visit daily Max's worst needs was tremendously depressing. To detail all of Max's problems with incontinence was draining and sad, not to mention putting on paper his diabolical health through each winter, as he was plagued by colds and chest infections, croup, and glue ear. I was so relieved when I managed to complete the application.

It was Louise who ended up helping us with the forms for Max. But it was still not right.

While the care and maintenance of Max's needs sometimes make me feel isolated, there are always good friends that can be called upon. Every Monday night since he was eight years old Max has attended a wonderful dance class run by the lovely Sarah. All the children who attend have DS, and over the years I have developed important relationships with all their mothers and fathers too. On a Monday evening, when all the regulars are deposited within the Cufos Centre near Alexandra Palace, some of the mothers meander back to Helen's house nearby. There is something lovely about it being so casual. Nothing is organised; we just know that during term time every Monday evening is dance time, and our chance to catch up for an hour.

Thinking about our get-togethers – over cups of tea or glasses of wine – it strikes me how little time we actually spend talking about our children. We hardly ever get into any discussions about them or their special needs. Obviously we do talk about some of the problems we are facing; we know we have such valuable support. However, just knowing that another adult is experiencing nearly the same difficulties as you – the same worries and fears, the same traumas and fights – can be a terrific comfort. And often that is all you need.

Four of us – Helen, Rebecca, Fiona and me – would probably never have met if our children did not have DS. Our children, Hannah, Robbie, Ophia and Max, are very different individuals. We never forget first and foremost that they are our children, just like anybody else's children; they just happen to have an additional gene. This gene manifests itself in many ways, but fundamentally we like to see them as our cherished children first, their disability second. I cannot speak for my friends, but I know that to come into contact with such special people on a weekly basis is a privilege. When we don't meet up, when it's the school holidays or Max is ill, I miss that contact and the rare camaraderie that only we can truly share. We respect each other's individual values and concerns, but are very united in our love for our children. Together we face the fear of what the future holds for our children. I'm sure everyone's view on the future for our children is very different, and that the aspirations and goals of one individual may differ widely from another's, but we still have that core knowledge that we are not alone.

Actually, what we do most is laugh. We tend to spend the entire hour relating funny, sometimes revoltingly obscene, stories to one another, enjoying the moment and basking in the fun of life. We are all similar, but at the same time we are all very individual and different. I cherish what we have. I don't take it for granted and am well aware that life is random and that it could evaporate in a moment. Within our group there is freedom to be ourselves, to not have to conform, and ultimately to have a bloody good laugh. It is a wonderful release.

When Max was almost 13, one of the other mothers from the dance class and I decided to create an off-shoot, a 'youth club' for the slightly older members. Christa and I could see that the teenage hormones had kicked in for one or two of the children. Christa's son, Raffy, and Max were certainly displaying all the classic signs of stroppy teenagers, along with all the baggage that goes with adolescence. Our aim was to provide an opportunity for these young people to enjoy each other's company in a less structured, but still safe environment. The aim was to give them the opportunity to 'chill and hang out', just like any other teenager. That's quite a hard thing to achieve and from the outset we went to some lengths to obtain other parents' views and opinions. We decided to hold our 'club' every other Friday after school and to share the venue between one another's houses. We started small with just four teenagers: Raffy, Annalie, Nikita and Max. Each host provides a bit of food and the adult in that house is responsible for the one and a half hours that the club runs.

Although this type of club was new territory for all of us, we had a general idea of how it should be run. We felt that, however tempting it may be, the adult should keep well away and allow the teenagers to feel unsupervised. Our children spend their lives being controlled and directed and for a large part of the time this is essential, but to show them respect and let them learn how to motivate and entertain themselves would be rewarding for all. People with DS are not great organisers; they will either willingly follow a given path, or stubbornly refuse, to the point of exasperation! Leaving them to think for themselves can be quite a challenge so it's far easier to pass through the room quickly and casually suggest a possible activity. But slowly, through time, we've all stopped interfering. Eventually, one of the teens will motivate the members into an activity all will enjoy. It can be agony to step back and not get involved, but it's essential.

They all love music, so this is always a major focus at the youth club, karaoke being the favourite. Snogging is also an ever-present feature. Whilst we all fidget nervously thinking about it and fret about the consequences, who are we to dictate? They too should know what it's like to enjoy the intoxicating highs and lows of flirting, to fall in and out of love, to have love thwarted and to have it gleefully returned. To wrestle with emotions like jealousy and desire, and to know those feelings are real and valid. By giving them some freedom we provide them with an opportunity to learn a moral code. It's interesting to hear them quickly berating one another if standards slip! Max has on the odd occasion tried to sneak a kiss from Annalie, who is 'going out' with Raffy; he's soon put in his place by Annalie or Nikita who remind him it's not right to kiss someone who's spoken for – even if Annalie doesn't seem to mind!

Each adult tries to share the glimpses of our children's behaviour, good or bad, that they are privileged to see. It's a rare treat to spy on our children socially interacting with one another, so this is an irresistible occasion to watch them secretly, if sometimes agonising.

Paul and I once watched Max display his extraordinarily bossy nature while attempting to organise cricket with his friends in the garden. We were appalled to witness our son dictate and lecture, unchallenged by the rest of the group! Not once throughout the entire game did Max let go of the bat or the ball!

At the time of writing the youth club has been going for two years and we have a new member, Hannah. It's hard work, but it's great. The best part about the youth club is watching Max get so excited beforehand. It was recently our turn to host, so Max rose to the occasion in true Max fashion. We started by clearing and cleaning the front room and then swiftly moved on to preparing the sandwiches. Max was terribly thorough with the electric carpet sweeper, even the downstairs toilet got a going over. He was in charge of microwaving the popcorn and putting all the dishes on to the table. I had to hide a smile, when halfway through artistically placing the Jaffa cakes on their plate, Max's hands flew to his face in alarm when he realised he had forgotten to change. He was still in his school uniform and this caused him great distress. He went tearing off upstairs to change into more appropriately 'cool' clothes, and reappeared in jeans and a T-shirt.

Max's enthusiasm can be delightful, but exhausting, and I heaved a sigh of relief when the doorbell rang to announce the first arrival. Max raced to the door to welcome his friends and I enjoyed watching him cluck and fuss over them. It is so important to let these gorgeous individuals experience the delights and the traumas of being a teenager. Such fleeting, but essential moments of private interaction with others can be overlooked, but they are the building blocks of life and we need him to experience and learn from them, just like everyone else.

Chapter Sixteen

11 May

Today at Max's school, Brenda, head of pastoral care, took me to one side to recount an amusing story she felt I must hear. Max had been busy in the sanctuary of the disabled toilets (he's nervous of the bigger boys) when he bellowed for Brenda. Word was soon passed up to the office and Brenda grabbed the set of clean clothes she keeps for such occasions and jogged down to Max, slightly nervous of what she might find. Brenda tapped gently on the toilet door to mark her arrival and Max let her in.

'Hi Max, you asked for me, is everything all right?'

'Hi Brenda, yes I'm fine thanks, I just thought you'd like to wipe my bottom.'

'That's very kind of you Max, but I'm sure you

can wipe your own bottom. But thanks for thinking of me!'

When Charlie arrived, I felt complete. That has everything to do with how I felt society viewed me, not how I viewed Max or Charlie. Perhaps it's a chink in my own armour, but I always felt patronised by others, particularly other mothers. Some had expressed unwanted sympathy to me, so perhaps it wasn't entirely in my head. Charlie's birth gave me confidence and strength; I never considered feeling guilty about how I felt. I welcomed it.

I view my children as totally separate entities. I'm proud of them in equal measures and, like a lioness protecting her cubs, would fight equally for them too. In my eyes Max is just as beautiful as his brother, inside and out. Any guilt I may carry is for Charlie since he has had no option but to embrace the circumstances he was born into.

The need for a bottomless pit of time and money is the practical reality of having Max. Is it something I resent or question? Not really: I'd be lying if I didn't admit to it being a massive drain on our resources as a family, but no parent would hesitate in making every effort to help and support their child and I'm no different.

Any parent must deal with balancing attention and financial generosity between siblings. Sibling rivalry is alive and kicking all over the world. Sometimes you just can't make it balance out. Even if you feel the equation is harmonious, your children invariably will not.

Charlie was three and Max five, when Paul and I celebrated our eighth wedding anniversary. We wanted to include the boys in our plans, so we took a Tweenies cake to Pizza Express and had a great time. Because they were so heavily into 'show and tell' at nursery school, I thought getting out my wedding dress would reinforce the whole explanation of our marriage. As I lay my stunning, bone-corseted dress out on the bed, a few leaves of confetti fell from the folds of cream silk. For a moment I was enveloped in nostalgia, but I was quickly brought back to reality by a familiar voice.

'You're a bit big for it now, Mummy.'

I say this, because from birth Charlie's always been razor-sharp. Very early on he sussed out the difference between Max and the rest of the world. I think this initially presented itself just by the extra attention Max received in the form of such enquiries as, 'Would Max like an ice cream?'

Such generosity towards Max seemed to manifest itself quite often. No one considered offering an ice cream to Charlie, he would get one by default, but he was perceptive to register the difference, even as a toddler.

I think Charlie felt invisible. I think he got angry. I think he decided to be uncompromising and go for what he most desired: his mother. He stuck to me like glue. If I was deep in conversation, he would crawl on to my lap and reach up to my chin with his chubby little hand, pulling my face around to meet his. He demanded my complete attention and got it. It's been that way ever since.

As time went by Charlie was quick to notice not just the obvious differences between him and his brother, like how he could run faster, climb trees or feed himself, but also the little things, like how Max always had a cold, how he was unable to use a knife and fork or pronounce words properly. Whilst he clocked up the differences pretty early on, he never pointed them out or asked why. He didn't know any different.

That's not to say Max's inadequacies haven't been highlighted to him by his peers. Towards the end of his time in primary school, Charlie received unwanted attention from certain individuals who would point out to him that his brother was a 'retard'. Or he would over-hear unpleasant comments made about Max, remarks that hurt him deeply.

When Charlie was about six, we explained to him

about the condition of Down's syndrome. He'd heard the word much earlier; people are remarkably insensitive to Charlie, freely discussing Max in front of him, just like he's not there. They still do. Charlie is a quiet, sensitive individual who runs deep. When we explained about DS we said that the creation of a person was a bit like making a cake and that when making Max, a bit too much sugar was added. Still a cake, but not quite as the recipe suggested. Charlie took this on board and could see the logic. I think he questioned why that should entitle Max to be offered such a lot of ice cream, but he never said.

Charlie and Paul are two peas in a pod, similar in looks and personality. Both are computer nerds and insanely passionate about cricket and music. In sharing mutual passions they've forged a close bond. That bond between father and son is even more evident in the rapport between Paul and Max. Whilst Charlie naturally turns to me in times of need, Max turns to Paul. It's a privilege to see such love and devotion between them.

Now that he's much older, Charlie and I are still just as close – he never let go of his fierce grip – and we have deep conversations about Max. I'm painfully honest, encouraging him to be the same. He has deep love for his brother and will be the first to rush up the stairs if a loud crash suggests Max has come to harm. I've seen him weep with worry for his brother and beam with pride. His sense of humour helps too. When Charlie was about nine and Max was 11, we went to the theatre to see *Joseph and The Amazing Technicolor Dreamcoat*. Before the show, we went for some supper in a nearby restaurant. Just before we left, Max declared he needed the toilet, so I accompanied him as he still required some supervision with this. To my horror I discovered that his poo was pesto green. After denying all knowledge of how this could be, Max trotted off back to our table. By the time I arrived the entire restaurant was aware that Max had green poo. Part of his charm is his breath-taking honesty and he had no qualms in proudly declaring the discovery in a loud voice to anybody who was happy to listen. Paul and I were trying to figure out what had happened when a small voice piped up, desperately trying not to giggle.

'I promised not to say anything, but I guess I should now.'

Charlie told us that he had spotted Max tucking into some bright green play-dough and was sworn to secrecy.

Charlie has a natural empathy towards people with special needs and to see such kindness and under-standing from his big heart fills me with pride. But there are times when Charlie can be forgiven for feeling frustration and rage towards his brother. Max traps us all. Visits to the park are few. Aside from the stares, Max will suddenly decide that he's had enough and want to return home. And whilst we try not to jump to his every whim, he will be disgracefully behaved until we make a move to leave. He'll sit on the floor, refusing to walk, or moan incessantly until we could all throttle him. Who'd want to go in the first place?

Charlie is older than his years. Perhaps he was just born that way, he certainly has an aura about him that suggests he's been here before, but I feel we are partly responsible. He's had little chance to enjoy the innocence of childhood. Whilst he's unaware of this now, I wonder whether as an adult he'll look back at these years with regret and resentment. Not long into his infancy there were moments that Paul and I would have preferred to hide from him, but we had little choice. Who would wish for any child to experience the acute embarrassment of their elder brother soiling himself in front of his friends? Who really wants to ask a child to always be the sensible one, to always be prepared to give way to a sometimes grumpy, ungrateful brother? Logically Charlie has always understood that his generous spirit is gratefully welcomed by me and Paul, but there are times when it must stick in his throat.

Charlie has a particularly warped view of brothers.

At times it seems that he feels that all fellow humans, particularly his peers, who do not have DS should be immaculately behaved. He can see no reason why their behaviour should be nothing short of perfect. If any of his friends behaves like Max sometimes does, Charlie becomes agitated and impatient. He cannot understand why they should behave childishly, outrageously, or rudely if they are bog-standard mortals. It does him no favours and we've gently introduced the concept that perhaps not every characteristic Max displays is due to his DS. Quite possibly only a tiny percentage of his behaviour is down to the condition. But for the moment Charlie's having none of it. He can often be heard saying, 'He's a pain in the neck.' He refuses to acknowledge that Max may just be an average brother, annoying and irritating at times, just like everyone else's.

Charlie is oblivious to his advanced maturity. He scoffs at any rebuke to his lack of humour or tolerance in certain situations and fakes his innocence when accused of being self-righteous. The poor chap is plagued by a few family traits, pedantry being one. But that said, he is also an adorable individual who is a delight to spend time with. He has adult perception and quick wit, as well as a bright mind and an engaging charm. And in most ways, Charlie behaves like any other boy of his age. He spends a great deal of time holed up in his room with the Red Hot Chili Peppers or Fountains of Wayne and his favourite treat is to spend an hour or two on a Saturday morning cruising through the children's books in WHSmiths or Waterstones. If he manages to get a book out of me, which he invariably does, and if we follow the purchase with a hot chocolate, then his morning is complete.

Charlie is also painfully forgetful, but at 11 that's a luxury he can afford. For now I simply relish the moments when I see him enjoying himself with pure abandonment, for that's what childhood is all about.

Chapter Seventeen

11 July

*Is life always to belt along at such a stressful pace?
Yesterday Charlie had to accompany me in the back
of an ambulance while Max was foaming at the
mouth, choking on a sausage. Charlie was so
terrified he refused to leave his brother and go in
the car with Paul.*

*Max had guzzled his supper with stunning speed,
without chewing and hardly pausing for breath. I
was bringing some drinks out from the kitchen,
having deposited the spaghetti and chopped sausage
in front of the boys only moments before. Max's
plate was already near to empty and he had turned
a most peculiar colour. He began to croak and wail,
waving his arm about. It scared the life out of us. I
managed to calm him down and ascertain that he
could still breathe, but he started to foam at the
mouth. In a panic we rang the hospital and they
sent an ambulance. Astonishingly it covered the*

distance from our house in Finchley to the Royal Free Hospital in less than 10 minutes. I have never felt so raw with fear. Both children clung to me like I had the power of a superhero.

They were waiting for us at casualty and we fell into their amazing, capable arms. With the sausage still stuck, they concluded that surgical removal was the only option, and I was signing consent forms for Max to go into theatre as Paul went with Max to have a pre-op X-ray to try and ascertain where the blockage was. During the X-ray Max relaxed for a split second when the radiologist asked him to slightly move his neck. The wretched sausage was displaced from the tight knit of muscles around his voice box. He swallowed and immediately bounced back to perfect health. After the delighted claps and cheers from all staff (including the ambulance men who asked if they could stay until he was okay), we collapsed on the floor with battle fatigue.

What particularly worries me is Charlie. No 10-year-old should have to witness that kind of trauma, all from gorging greedily on an innocent pasta supper.

The intense, high-pitched stress which accompanied us almost daily wore us down. Thus our interest was piqued when we were told about a hotel in

Cornwall, designed to cater exclusively for families with children. One of Max's pre-school teachers, Hilary Soloman, had been there with her young children and described it so enthusiastically, we felt compelled to investigate. The thought of being able to throw everything to cover all eventualities into the car was a luxury. Whilst the cost of our week's stay was no less than jumping on a plane to a sunny destination, the fact that we would not have the uncertainty and hassle that comes with holidaying abroad gave us enough incentive to undertake the five-hour drive to Cornwall.

For any poor, unsuspecting, childless soul who innocently books a holiday at The Bedruthan Steps Hotel, it must be a shock to discover that the hotel is set up purely to accommodate the dreams and demands of children and their exhausted parents. To arrive and be greeted by swarms of babies and toddlers all squealing with delight, as they rush from Jungle Tumble to Mark's Ark, must be a nightmare.

But for us with children, to be greeted by such incredible recreational activities, specifically designed for your little bundles of mayhem, is wonderful. Let's face it: if your children are happy, then you are happy. The heady mix of child facilities and the breathtaking Cornish coastline created a serene haven of tranquillity.

The hotel was built into the overhanging cliffs, so that it appeared suspended over the beach below. Just the smell of the sea, the sand and the sight of blanket upon blanket of heather, was an immediate pick-me-up. I felt I'd been transported directly to heaven. With entertainment in constant supply, just about any parental concern soon evaporates. For the first time ever, Paul and I had some degree of control over our day, managing to find some much-overdue respite. After one week at the hotel I actually started to laugh again. My normal bubbly giggle that had long since deserted me, so long in fact that I forgot I possessed it, returned.

We loved it so much, and it provided such valuable recuperation for us all, that we returned annually for four years. It was incredible how much just a few days rest dramatically changed the whole atmosphere within the family. We all got so much out of the break in more ways than we could have imagined. While the hotel was busy and always completely full, there was a refreshing feeling of space and freedom. Nobody trespassed on your personal space and a mutual understanding between parents was quickly established, particularly in any public areas. Paul and I relished the solitude. We did not crave entertainment or amusement and welcomed some time to chill out with one another.

The Bedruthan Steps Hotel also provided a venue for

Max to exercise his showmanship. By now he was well on the way to exploding with the enthusiasm of a true performer. Every night in the ballroom he would be right at the front, amongst the action, strutting his funky stuff. Any opportunity to grab the microphone and perform one of his 'standards' was gleefully snatched. You couldn't miss Max, not because he had DS, but because his zest for life and enjoyment of other people's praise always brought him to the forefront of any activity.

Max is a remarkable barometer when it comes to gauging what people are really like. Their behaviour towards him is often a very good indication as to how healthy their attitudes are. It is fascinating to watch children around him. Very quickly you can establish who are the healthy-minded, well-balanced individuals. It means you can retreat from those people who cannot cope with someone like Max. Free spirits who welcome anyone, in all shapes and sizes, are generally easy to spot: people like Daniel and Alexander, two young boys who were so kind to Max and stuck out to me like a couple of Belisha beacons. For days I watched them be kind, generous and delightful towards both my boys. Their behaviour impressed me so much that I felt I had to mention it to their parents, Brian and Stacey Rosenberg.

Brian is an impressive character, both physically and intellectually. Stacey, whilst much quieter, is the lynch-pin of their family. One morning I walked past as they were enjoying breakfast and Brian was juggling his youngest son Oliver on his knee. I was unable to resist pausing for a few moments to tell him how charming his children were. Brian's chest visibly rose, bursting with pride. We got talking and our two families began a very special relationship. From then on, any hope of peace and tranquillity was dashed, replaced by a welcome glimpse into the supportive and humorous life of the Rosenbergs. As families go we could not be more different, yet we gelled immediately.

One evening while we were engrossed in listening to Brian explain his thoughts on several of the world's current crises, I had the strangest feeling that I was being watched. I can't explain it but it just felt odd. I thought no more about it until the next evening when I had the same weird feeling. I chastised myself for being delusional. It turned out I wasn't. The next day in Jungle Tumble, Ruth grasped the courage to approach us. Ruth was the midwife who had delivered Max. He had been the first baby she had delivered with DS. She was the one who chose to spend time with me, not through a professional obligation, but simply because she is a lovely person. Then life got in the way and over the years we lost touch. Ruth went on to marry and have her own family, continuing to be a nurse and never forgetting Max. Max's outrageous performances had got her thinking. It took her a few days to feel bold enough to ask if it really was us.

Apparently it was Paul whom she recognised. Me, she wasn't so sure about. As well as looking very different in terms of hair and weight, I was also emotionally in a pretty bad way at the time of Max's birth, which tends to change you. Now I look back at photographs and can hardly recognise myself. I don't believe in coincidences and feel some events in life just marry up and happen for a reason. It was astonishing and quite wonderful to meet up with Ruth again. For her to see Max thriving, enjoying life at full throttle, was important since she had, after all, brought him into the world.

Holidays are places to plan and dream and it was on one of these trips to Cornwall that I began to envisage what it would be like to follow a few dreams of my own. Both boys were now at school and I dearly wished to return to some kind of work. I gave up my career when Max was born, and I was only too aware that a return to a demanding environment such as insolvency was totally out of the question. However, I felt that to explore another avenue of work could be an exciting possibility. I had always had a keen interest in hairdressing. From my early teens I would happily snip away at any willing volunteer's hair, cutting and creating new styles with naive confidence. I loved it and remembered my feelings of elation when I got it right and my victim was clearly delighted. I decided to sign up for a two-year course at Barnet College to take an HND in hairdressing. I was hoping I could work the college timetable around the boys' school hours.

Suddenly I was excited: I had wild dreams of qualifying and opening up my own salon, developing a fantastic range of hair products and generally being an overnight success! The start of college, though, was an almighty shock to my system. Being out of full-time education for a few decades left me stunned at how badly we were treated by the college. There was no mutual respect and most of the time the students were treated like cattle. Petty rules and inflexible attitudes left me irritated and frustrated. But I loved the course and enjoyed the company of all the other aspiring hairdressers. My classmates were a vibrant and motley crew, the majority of whom were in their late teens. Although I wasn't the only mature student, they were taken aback when they asked me my age. It was a sobering moment when one or two of them remarked that their mothers were the same age as me!

The whole family was energised about my course and

I felt well supported by Paul and my little boys. It was a bit tight, but I managed to leave college each day and dash to pick up the boys from school. My homework bled into the weekends, but Paul generously rose to the occasion by taking charge of the boys and whisking them off somewhere exciting like the cinema or the zoo. All went well for some time, until the headaches that have plagued me my entire life started to interfere with the routine to such an extent that I was forced to take days off sick.

In hindsight I was expecting too much from my life, dreaming of goals I could never realistically achieve. The tight turn-around I had negotiated and the ever-increasing burden of two little boys, who were each a healthy handful, proved too much. Without question they were my top priority and I had no problem in understanding that. When I say burden, I mean the day-to-day maintenance that any mother can identify with. The headaches began to become worse and unfortunately they were not the only hindrance. My depression returned with a vengeance. I was exhausted and unable to juggle the demands of family life with the hair-dressing course, which made me stressed and anxious. Something had to give and I had no hesitation in pulling out from my course. I knew without question that the care of my children was paramount, but I was dreadfully disappointed all the same.

I think I may have stopped the course just in time: I quickly realised that I had pushed the limits of my capabilities. Reluctantly I returned to the Charter Nightingale Hospital to see Dr Epen. This time I felt I had no option but to try medication; I had to see whether it could win the battle with the black dog that plagued me. This time I felt my situation was slightly different from before. I was very ill and I no longer had the luxury of being able to hide my bleak moods and paralysing listlessness from my children as I had done when they were babies and small toddlers. Max and Charlie had required care and attention, but mainly all they needed was lots of love and cuddles. Now they were older and more perceptive and there was no way I could carry off some kind of pretence. Any attempt at fooling them would quickly be discovered.

I'd also come around to acknowledging the merits of medication, losing my fear. I'd always kept an ear open to any information on mental health, and I discovered that there were important benefits to taking medication and I should perhaps welcome them, rather than hastily brush them aside. If I dismissed any chemical intervention, I would never know if I could be helped in this way. I knew I was kidding myself if I thought I could struggle on in my current condition, without any help, whether through therapy or medication.

I resumed my counselling sessions with Dr Epen and she enthusiastically jumped at the chance to try me on medication. She had always expressed her confidence in the benefits of antidepressants; it had always been me who had refused. I started on 25 mg of Sertraline, one of the commonly used antidepressant drugs (SSRIs). Very quickly I felt quite disgusting, life was a real effort comparable to trudging through treacle. This is a common reaction when these antidepressants are initially taken since they take time to bond with your chemistry. It was truly horrible: I was lethargic and vacant. I went back to Dr Epen every two to three weeks and each time the medication was gradually increased. It felt like an eternity, but eventually, at an alarmingly high dosage of 200 mg, my head began to clear. I no longer felt sluggish and I began to feel more in control of my dark desperate moods and more optimistic. A daily 200 mg dose of Sertraline is high and, as a precaution, I would have a blood test every three to four months to check my liver and kidney function. Whilst this was tedious and unpleasant, it went a long way to alleviating any concerns that kept popping into my head. And, of course, all the while, though being strongly discouraged, I continued to drink.

For as long as I can remember I have always got up in the middle of the night to pee. Very soon after starting the Sertraline these nightly visits became quite a chore. Although my bladder was full, I found it almost impossible to urinate. I would have to force myself awake and concentrate intently on connecting my brain thoughts to my bladder. Eventually I would be successful, but there were other changes affecting my body chemistry, which I found alarming. I developed a raging thirst, my hair thinned quite considerably and orgasms became a distant memory. However, there was a positive trade-off: my mental health was better and I became able to function more than adequately within my family. Throughout all my mishaps with my mental health, I was continuing to exercise every day if possible. By now Paul and I had swapped our miniature dolly cottage in Hampstead Garden Suburb for a spacious four-bedroom Georgian house in Finchley. I cheerfully took to pounding the streets of Finchley and started to embrace a kind of normality.

My confidence blossomed to such an extent that I failed to remember the hardship I had faced when trying to juggle college and my family. I have always been a creative person and am unable to resist customising items of clothing: I would feel much happier knowing that I had changed an item, making it unique. For a long time I had been drawn to adorning shoes and handbags with silk flowers. These would not be cheap, crude creations but beautiful, breathtakingly realistic – and expensive – ones!

With the extra room we had in our new house, I hatched a plan to enjoy my creativity and incorporate it into a business. *So Gorgeous Ltd* was born and I just loved it. I sank my heart into every bespoke design and happily plunged into the PR and marketing until I had a classy website cleverly created by Paul, and an exciting range of vibrant shoes and handbags. I did everything myself: sourcing, buying, and physically hand sewing all my designs. With a few features in *You Magazine*, the *Express* and the *Telegraph* I was well on the way to nurturing what could have been a successful business.

Once again, just at my most intense period of juggling work and family life, I paid the price with recurring headaches. For a few months I was forced to abandon my daily run: I could no longer sustain such a routine and, to be honest, I couldn't afford the time. The benefits of passing up my run allowed me a few more valuable hours to work during the day when my children were at school. But the consequence of this daily omission was harsh: I began to put on weight at an alarming rate. By this time I had been on Sertraline for three years. The available literature suggests that weight gain is minimal for the first two years. After that, depending on the individual metabolism, weight gain can become an issue, and it certainly did with me. I feel I dropped the ball the minute I let my regular exercise slip and from then on, no matter what I did, no matter what diet I tried, even doubling the exercise I resumed, I just got fatter and fatter. This continued for nearly a year until once again, I felt compelled to drop some component from my hectic schedule. I knew realistically that component could only be *So Gorgeous*, even though it broke my heart.

Another clear decision manifested itself almost simultaneously. Along with *So Gorgeous*, I also had to stop taking Sertraline. Putting on so much weight truly terrified me. I felt I had absolutely no control over my body and therefore my life. *So Gorgeous* had bled into my life to such an extent that I would find myself sneaking off upstairs to my office at the slightest opportunity and crossing that line between children and work that I swore I would never do. Suddenly I felt like I'd put my children way down the list of my priorities and for me that had to change.

Before making the decision to stop, I did have a discussion with Dr Epen and my GP about the unwanted side effects I was experiencing and whether another brand of antidepressant would help. They both felt that the high dose I required would make it almost inevitable that any type of SSRI would have similar side effects, particularly weight gain. At the time, I was unpleasantly preoccupied with the amount of weight I was carrying. I was very overweight, none of my clothes would fit and I felt disgusting. I put a great deal of effort into dieting and exercise, but I continued to gain weight, rather than lose it. I found this terrifying. When you start on the path of medication, there is always an open discussion about when the time will be right to come off. I was never prescribed antidepressants with the intention of being on them for life so for me the time to stop had arrived.

Coming off Sertraline was seriously tough. I'm not against medication, but I feel it needs to be approached with caution and a healthy respect. And I have no particular war with drug companies, but I was enormously frustrated and enraged by the complete lack of support made available to individuals attempting to come off antidepressants. I cut quite a hysterical sight in the morning, bleary-eyed, swearing profusely, wielding a sharp Stanley knife. In order to reduce the dose, I was desperately trying to split my chalky tablets into reasonable, consistently sized pieces. In the same way you gradually introduce the medication into your system, you must gradually remove it, only much slower. Otherwise you may (depending on the individual, of course) suffer a number of side effects, including any or all of these:

nausea, stomach gripes, diarrhoea, muscle spasms, headaches, sweating and an inability to concentrate.

I decided it would be wise not to embark on this whole withdrawal process alone. The best help I felt I could employ would be my wonderful homeopath, Jane Harter. She was fantastic, providing me with moral support as well as homeopathic remedies. I also spent a great deal of time walking, literally walking the Sertraline out of my system. I would drag on my battered trainers, plug myself into my iPod and walk for hours, marching up and around Alexandra Palace, Muswell Hill and the length and breadth of Finchley. Eventually when I was down to a relatively tiny daily dose, I suddenly became terribly brave and defiant. After visiting Jane (by now, I almost used her as a coun- sellor, rather than a homeopath) I walked home, walked through the door and without pausing for breath, searched the entire house for every last remaining tablet of Sertraline. I emptied every handbag and every drawer and by the time I had finished, I had a small stockpile of white tablets collected in a terracotta pot. I dragged Paul outside, poured us both a glass of red wine and lit a ceremonial fire in the terracotta pot. We both watched as the last of the Sertraline burnt to dust. Drawing a line of fire through the process gave me an overwhelming sense of relief, and I suddenly felt more in control.

Naturally my problems did not stop there. It took a full year for all of the Sertraline to leave every organ in my body and not surprisingly my depression began to visit regularly. I've now tried to stop drinking – completely! This really is quite an achievement for me as I just adore my daily glass of wine. But finally, after years of being told that alcohol is a depressant, and not such a good idea for me, I've accepted the view that perhaps it's true, and I can no longer afford to live my life governed by demons. I guess whatever I can do to reduce the threat of anything sabotaging my mental health is worth considering, even if that means forgoing some of life's little luxuries, however pleasurable!

Chapter Eighteen

21 February

We are so fed up with Max. His behaviour today has left us feeling exhausted and dreadfully low, even if we are on holiday in Dubai. I have such fears for Charlie. I don't know how he stands it in this family. My biggest worry is that he will run a mile from us just as soon as he can. I just hope it's not Australia.

We decided on a family day out, well, morning really, best not to push it. We all wanted to go and take a look at the ski resort we're told has just opened here. How incredible is that, a ski resort with real snow, smack bang in the middle of the desert! I know we can't use it, but I have to check this out, just to see it with my own eyes. With any luck we can get a spot of lunch and pretend we're in the Alps!

Just before we go down to the lobby to catch the hotel minibus, Max declares that he doesn't want to go to the ski resort. He says he wants to go to the gold souk. Gold souk my arse, he hasn't a clue what the gold souk is; he just wants to pull rank and be difficult. Paul has a chat and explains that, as a family, we all want to check out the ski resort, and that we have plans (as he well knows) to go to the gold souk another day.

We all get on the bus and we feel optimistic. Looks like it could be fun as well as interesting. The ski resort juts out of one side of the shopping mall, like a gigantic aluminium Thermos flask. It can be seen from anywhere in Dubai it's so enormous. We arrive at the Mall of The Emirates and enter via the escalators. At the top is a wall made entirely of mirrors. In our reflection I spot a large wet patch on Max's trousers. How stupid of us to think we could have come out not expecting the worst. Dropped the ball again. We have no spare clothes, so have to make a detour to the supermarket. Charlie is mortified beyond words; every passer-by spots Max's wet patch and his Down's syndrome. Perfect: a double whammy. We are speechless with embarrassment. A trail of stares follows us, all the way to the supermarket. Thankfully clothes here are so cheap. I pick up new shoes, new socks, pants and trousers, all for a tenner. By now Max is dripping.

By way of some humble apology (which falls short),
I tell Charlie he can choose a bar of chocolate.

After we complete our purchases, Max and Paul
go off to the toilets to change. Charlie and I wait,
for what seems like for ever. Soon the pair emerge
from the loos and we make our way to the ski
resort, planning lunch as we go. Then the smell hits
us, letting us know Max has done a poo in his
pants. Thankfully I have bought two of everything.
We return to the toilets for another change. Charlie
is now crying. I feel so bad for him. He starts to tell
me how angry Max is making him feel and, to be
honest, I can't blame him. I cannot believe Max has
had two accidents in the space of half an hour. I dig
deep, to suggest to myself that he may be finding it
difficult to adjust to the heat. In truth, I have a
sneaky suspicion that he is doing this on purpose.
It's his way of demonstrating that he wants to be in
charge. I feel sick with disappointment. The day is a
disaster.

Finally we arrive at the ski resort. It's fabulous,
quite amazing. After lengthy and protracted sign
language with the staff, we establish we cannot go
inside without being fully kitted out, ready to ski.
Charlie is desperate to go in, not to ski, but just to
see. Max is determined he's not going within a mile

of it. Charlie doesn't want to split the family up and go in with just one of us, so we compromise. We all agree to have lunch, overlooking a glass window giving us a small peek of the snowy white mountains inside.

Max wets himself again. I could cry and so, I think, could Paul. Charlie is crying and very, very angry. Paul and Max disappear into the toilets to salvage what is left of Max's outfit, while I cuddle Charlie and blindly search for some way to make things right for him.

My head says it's wrong, but my heart tells me to do it anyway: Paul and I decide to fork out for a portable PlayStation for Charlie. He's been twittering on and on about one for weeks, and we can pick one up here for a reasonable price. The smile on Charlie's face says it all, and I hope that, for just a little while, we have made up for a truly disgusting day.

When Max was a toddler, we went to a meeting, which was being held in a Portakabin within the grounds of a primary school. It was a hot day and the meeting lasted about an hour. When we came out, Max saw a dog tied up outside the cabin. Before I could stop him, he'd rushed over to say hello. Max loves dogs and wishes with all his heart that he could have one of his own. This was a perfect opportunity to indulge one of his passions. The poor dog had been tied up outside in the heat for over an hour, and, not surprisingly, was hot, thirsty and distressed. Max bent down to pat the dog. It was not particularly large, rather like a medium-sized Lassie. The dog went ballistic, and jumped up at Max, growling and ready to bite. Thankfully Max was not bitten, but he was badly frightened. I really feel it wasn't the dog's fault, but sadly the attack has left Max very nervous of dogs. He still loves them and hankers after a Dalmatian, but if we are out and a dog barks he gets terribly worried. I believe this incident has been the trigger to a number of phobias that have plagued Max throughout his life. As the years go by they are getting worse.

Max has developed a genuine phobia of clowns. Most days he is a drama queen, and has been known to fake emotion to gain attention, but his fear of clowns is quite disturbing. He turns deathly white and immediately loses control of his bladder; he is immobilised and dreadfully fearful. No amount of reassurance can bring him around. This fear of clowns can also bleed into other areas of 'dressing up'. He is petrified of such so-called 'child friendly' Disney-like characters, animal outfits and Father Christmas. In fact any costume harbouring a human is traumatic for him. His fear has ruined many a family day out. Even the giant teddy bear, innocently passing out adverts for a local pizza restaurant, is an enemy.

One particular incident will be ingrained in my memory for life. For his eighth birthday, Charlie chose to go to *The Lion King* at the Lyceum Theatre. With great excitement we all trooped into the West End, having heard some fabulous things about the show. Within minutes of the breathtaking opening scene – in which herds of colourful animals of every shape and colour noisily migrate on to the stage – Max was up and out of his seat, in a panic. It was too much for him and he accidentally wet himself, so Paul took him outside to change him and try to calm him down. After that he refused to return to his seat. Through a bit of sign language from the auditorium doors, I managed to establish that Paul was staying out in the foyer with Max. At the interval we swapped and I took my place at the front of house for the second half of the show. The staff were terribly kind, inviting us to go downstairs to a bar area where some of the actors, dressed in their glorious animal costumes, were waiting for their cue to go onstage. One actor, who was a rather ravishing hyena, made a great deal of time for Max, demonstrating to him that he was just a bloke in a furry coat and trousers. Max loved this, and was hugely impressed from an actor's point of view, but I still couldn't get him to put his phobia to one side and go back to watch the show. Poor Charlie was forced to watch the entire performance with one or other of us, knowing that once again, Max had grabbed the limelight, even on his birthday.

Another of Max's fears is the metal detector at airports. Our big trip to Dubai came about after we got rather brave and decided to risk getting on a plane. An old school friend of mine recommended the place; he had been out there on business a few times and found it to be ideal for families. Everyone was very welcoming, the streets were safe and the beaches were clean and glorious so we thought we'd give it a try. With a similar budget to what we spent in Cornwall, we booked a week's stay at the Jumeirah Beach Hotel (the one shaped like a wave). We had been told that all the bedrooms were gigantic, and could easily accommodate the four of us. Best of all, the hotel was right next door to the Wild Wadi, the largest water park in the world.

We arrived at Heathrow in plenty of time and slowly made our way through check-in and passport control. Wherever we go, the kindness of one or two people will always stand out. On this occasion one particular security guard spotted Max and greeted him with cheerful enthusiasm, engaging him in conversation and generally being quite lovely. We were in the queue and it was soon our turn to place all our hand luggage on to the conveyor belt so it could go through the X-ray machines. We were in no rush, and the atmosphere was good, so we had no warning of what was to come. The next step was to walk through the metal detector whereupon Max threw an almighty wobbly. Unfortunately I had gone through the machine first and set it off with my belt buckle. It beeped aggressively and something in Max's brain flipped. We just couldn't get him to go through the machine. By now his anxiety had led him to have an accident, which was clearly visible on the floor.

I stood there wishing for the ground to swallow me up. Max was wailing, Charlie was mortified, and Paul and I went into damage control overdrive. The entire occasion was played out in front of a sizeable audience who, understandably, wanted us swiftly out of the way. The staff were calm and professional but unless Max went through the machine, or allowed one of the security guards to go over him with a hand-held metal detector, we were going nowhere. The friendly security guard who had been chatting to Max earlier emerged from behind the conveyor belt. He calmly introduced himself again, shook Max's hand and asked if he might check Max over with the metal detector. Amazingly

Max agreed. I think he was momentarily thrown by this man's gentle manner and felt safe. Thankfully the check was made, and we were given the all clear, leaving a puddle behind us. I felt so guilty and embarrassed and offered to clear up the mess, but we were sent on our way by the charming and delightful security staff.

The 'pull-ups' came out after that. Max hated wearing them, but Paul and I were not taking any chances. The flight was mercifully short and we arrived in Dubai close to midnight. Once we got off the plane and were working our way down the labyrinth of escalators we began to take in our new destination. Dubai is a symphony of gold and glass. It is very modern but it is a country based on Arabic culture, which meant people were dressed very differently to anything Max had seen before. As we were going down the final staircase to reclaim our baggage, Max loudly declared that he was frightened of the *shepherds*. Paul and I were already mildly apprehensive about visiting a country that we knew very little about culturally and Max's outburst seemed to confirm our worst fears. The fear of our holiday being over before it had even started made me feel sick. We stopped and Paul quietly took Max to one side, and slowly and clearly explained to him all about the *shepherds*. He told him that this style of clothing was how people dressed in this country and as visitors we must show them the utmost respect. Thankfully the message went in, and we had no further problems with the way the *shepherds* dressed.

Paul's small speech had such a positive impact that Max embraced the holiday and all the new routines (which he normally hates) with praiseworthy merit. It is terribly hard for him to adjust to any new environment. Often it is easier and less stressful if we stick to something familiar – hence our four-year annual pilgrimage to Cornwall. But sometimes life is just not that simple. As a family we have to deviate from the norm occasionally and do new things, especially for Charlie's sake. Otherwise we may all go mad.

The next morning we enthusiastically made our way over to the Wild Wadi. We had high hopes that the visit would go smoothly. The water park was simply fantastic. The boys thought all their dreams had come true and they soon conquered every ride in the park. So much so, that Max had the confidence to make some runs on his own. This was highly unusual, not only because he was plagued by his own fears and phobias but also from a practical, safety point of view. However, we soon realised that the Wild Wadi has lifeguards at every turn who are bright and enthusiastic. Before long Max had introduced himself to practically every lifeguard in the park. They were brilliant, treating him with friendship and warmth, which in turn gave him the confidence to enjoy a new experience: independence. I'm very aware that the whole holiday was madly unreal, but for times during that one week, we found a kind of paradise.

While we were away, Max complained of a sore tooth. I checked his mouth and indeed the gum area surrounding one of his teeth appeared swollen and inflamed. I cannot fully explain how I feel when something like this happens. A small hysteria seems to start in my feet and work its way up through my body. Although I do my utmost to remain calm and try to relax, I visibly shake. Max just cannot risk having a problem with his teeth or getting infected gums. Because of the hole in his heart, he has to be extra careful with his gums, otherwise the infection could seize the opportunity to take the direct route to his heart.

On our return from Dubai we were straight round to our dentist, Mr Bird. Mr Bird has been Max's dentist since he had his operation at the Eastman Dental Hospital. He has a brilliant way with Max, which is not surprising since most of Mr Bird's patients are children or adults with special needs. He has huge empathy for his patients but at the same time suffers no nonsense. When Max first arrived at the clinic he would freak at the slightest thing, in particular the electronic chair.

Mr Bird respected this and at each visit would patiently introduce some new procedure, be it slightly moving the electronic chair or turning the overhead light on. Max is still cautious and suspicious about the dentist, but with Mr Bird I feel we have a reasonable chance of getting his cooperation.

Thankfully, this wasn't going to be a major crisis. A small piece of baby tooth left behind from a molar was working its way out of his gums and causing an inflammation. Mr Bird prescribed some gel to alleviate the problem and we were set free and sent on our way.

Chapter Nineteen

3 June

Max is particularly cheesed off with me today. He is so angry with me he cannot bear to look me in the eye. Whilst the feeling is uncomfortable, I must admit to feeling rather gleeful. For once I am one step ahead of him, a very rare occurrence at the moment. Max is on a bread ban for today. Last night he was outrageously obnoxious. I got to two and three quarters in the countdown to the bread ban, but he just couldn't get himself together. He wasn't being asked to perform an outrageously mean task, oh no, just turn the telly off, get off his backside and have a shower. So today, much to his disgust, he's not having toast. It's cereal for breakfast and a salad for lunch at school. He took plenty of food: egg mayonnaise and tuna mayonnaise salad, banana and yoghurt. Just a bit too healthy for Max's taste, and lacking his all-important, beloved sandwiches. I've

*had to be one step ahead and I've rung the school to
tell them, no, he has not forgotten to bring his
sandwiches, and no, his parents are not starving him,
his healthy lunch is quite correct. They laughed and
said they'd warn the dinner ladies. That boy can
charm the birds from the trees, and I wouldn't put it
past him to have at least one gullible soul passing
him a sausage roll in sympathy. Boy, is he going to
be mad at me tonight.*

The temptation to sneak another doughnut was strong, and resisting it was pure agony. I only managed to restrain myself because if I give in, Max will want one. That is something I must avoid at all costs, since a doughnut is the last thing he needs. We steadfastly adhere to a healthy-eating regime; Max has a low-functioning thyroid and a slow metabolism, which is common to people with DS. Therefore, having doughnuts so readily available is a very unusual occurrence, but this day is not really a day you could classify as normal. Today we are sitting on the steps of a Georgian house where Max is involved in filming *Notes on a Scandal* with Judi Dench, Cate Blanchett and Bill Nighy. We're about four weeks into the filming schedule and as Max dashes inside after being told that they're ready for the next scene, I find myself

wondering how on earth we got here? It's quite astonishing that Max should be in a film and I find I often
have to pinch myself as a reality check. It's hard to
believe such a stroke of luck should have come his way
and I am so thrilled for him.

The day of Max's audition for the film was quite
surreal. It's not every day that your son has the opportunity of meeting a film director such as Richard Eyre;
we were thrilled and proud. Bearing in mind that Max
will perform at the drop of a hat, his reputation as an
impressive performer had been firmly established in and
around North London. It was not just the stage at
Chickenshed that had benefited from his enchanting
ego; many a front room, school hall or back seat of a
car had been given the 'Max experience'. So when the
casting agents called me, it was no surprise to learn that
they had been given Max's name by quite a few sources,
all recommending that they see him.

Originally it was just to be Max and Paul going, but
my mum convinced me that this was a special moment
and that I would regret it later if I wasn't with him. She
was so right. As the auditions were being held in some
studios in Leicester Square, it seemed sensible to take
the Tube, straight down on the Northern Line, no
changes. Max was extremely hyped up and beside
himself with excitement. I was thrilled for him, but as a

parent I was also mindful of disappointment, so I kept myself in check. We arrived at the studios and I felt rather like part of Max's posse. The three of us sat opposite a few people auditioning for various other parts and they looked as nervous as I felt.

Soon we were asked to go through to meet Richard Eyre and the Casting Director, Maggie Lunn. We were made to feel very welcome and no eyebrows were raised as we trotted along to a room towards the back of the building. It was set up for the audition with a camera ready to film. Richard and Maggie were sat waiting. From the moment we walked through the door, the audition belonged to Max and he grabbed it with both hands. Paul and I sat at the back of the room, deliberately distancing ourselves from Max as he took up the invitation to sit at the table with Richard and Maggie. His energy and enthusiasm were bouncing off the walls. He couldn't stop talking and gave a gushing account of his love of the theatre, and everything he could sing, which he proceeded to do with gusto. Max wanted this part, and, all credit to him, he went into that room and gave everything he had. As Maggie acknowledged later, he just blew them away.

There were parts of the audition that had my toes curling in pure agony; he was so over the top. Richard and Maggie didn't really have to say a great deal to

Max. All they had to do was push a button and he was off like a rocket. They smiled a lot and seemed to like him, but you never know. I had serious concerns that he had presented himself as a precocious extrovert who would never shut up! The next few days were agony; we had good feedback from the casting agent, but we knew we had to be very careful with Max's fragile ego, and not forget that he is still a child. Eventually the call came through that a video of his audition had been couriered to New York for Scott Rudin, one of the producers, who would give the final word. It wasn't long before we heard: he was in! He had been chosen to play Ben in *Notes on a Scandal,* a Hollywood movie being filmed in England. I was filled to bursting with pride. Nothing could wipe the smile off my face that day.

Film sets are noted for their catering and Max will jump at the chance to eat. He lives for food with the result that, at age 13, he is worryingly overweight. This is partly because of DS and is compounded by his low-functioning thyroid, so life can be fraught when faced with such temptation as it was on the previous day when they were filming a scene involving a Christmas meal.

It had been one of the hottest days of the year in the UK and this was compounded by the lights and camera equipment that took up most of the space in the house.

As you can imagine it was unbearably hot. Suddenly Richard Eyre shouted 'Action', and the crew, hair and make-up ladies and I squeezed into tiny gaps we managed to find in the hallway. The actors, dressed in their winter cardigans and woollen jackets, were doing their best not to show any effects of the heat as they sat down in the dining room to enjoy the traditional Christmas meal, in all its glory – under lights.

After the fourth take it occurred to me that a good deal of replacement food was being delivered by the catering crew camped out in the next-door neighbour's kitchen. One of the hair and make-up ladies perceptively voiced my exact thoughts: 'Good Lord, who is actually eating this stuff?' Then it struck me – oh no, Max! Max was eating the food. How idiotic of me not to pre-empt such a disaster! Each take had involved him robustly tucking into his Christmas platter. Although it was acting, Max was embracing the moment with unequivocal enthusiasm and practically clearing his plate each time! It was not long before he was well and truly stuffed and ready to blow. All I could do now was imagine the likely outcome, a thought that made me break out in a cold sweat. I didn't have long to wait.

'That's it! I've had enough, I want my mum and I want to go home.' I could hear him quite clearly, even from the hallway, and I knew we were in for a rocky afternoon.

I went in to where the drama was unfolding and grabbed his sweaty little hand. We made our way to the basement flat put aside for Max, which was equipped with a telly and DVD player and was lovely and cool. Sadly any paraphernalia that had been installed to distract Max in moments of boredom or anguish were completely useless on this occasion. Max had well and truly blown a gasket and I saw no way of pulling him back. Meanwhile shooting had come to a grinding halt and Judi, Bill, Cate and the rest of the cast and crew were forced to sweat it out in the blistering heat, staring at their congealed roast potatoes and soggy vegetables.

The crew on the film were wonderful. No fuss was made, and although I felt embarrassed, no pressure was placed on me to get my child to cooperate. Thank goodness, because he was immovable. His stubborn streak had taken over, and I knew I was doomed. There was only one thing for it. I would have to play my final card, which I kept hidden up my sleeve for a dire emergency: call in Paul. Paul and Max have a mutual adoration thing going on, which I love to watch. I summoned Paul who, thankfully, was only a few miles away in Hendon. Within 20 minutes he was parked up and in full persuasion mode with Max. I was left wondering whether I should be worried that all the crew would think Paul and I forced Max into performing in this film, or pretend nothing out of the ordinary had happened and bury my head in the sand. Either way he had delayed filming by at least an hour, and the precious filming budget must have been haemorrhaging at a frightening rate as the cast and crew stood around waiting.

Paul's sterling work brought Max to a place where he agreed to see the day's filming to a conclusion. He arrived back on set to the warm embrace of all the actors, who were patiently waiting for him. Judi Dench made a generous and probably truthful comment that Max was only acting out what they all were really feeling. Everyone was mighty hot and would have preferred to be at home sipping an ice-cold drink in the cool shade!

In fairness to Max, when he agreed to play the part of Ben, he had no real concept of what filming would be like. All the acting he had performed had been in Chickenshed's theatre and all the acting he had seen had been in films for children, or in the theatre. He adores theatre, we make sure that he sees every West End performance, and he loves all the singing and dancing. He has all the CDs of *Chitty Chitty Bang Bang*, *Mary Poppins*, *Joseph*, *Mamma Mia!*: the list is endless. At his audition for the film Max was delighted to discover that Richard Eyre was the director of the stage production of *Mary Poppins*. Max immediately broke into song with an enthusiastic rendition of 'A Spoonful of Sugar'. I think it came as a slight shock when he realised that the filming he was to do on *Notes on a Scandal* was of a more serious nature and would not involve singing.

We needed to explain to Max that he had committed to a project and it would be most unprofessional to pull out. Perhaps he was disappointed that the part wasn't as exciting as he would have wished, but it was *proper* acting, something that Max not only showed a talent for, but a true passion as well. The added bonus, of course, was that he was to be paid. Max having his own money was quite a new concept, so when we suggested that perhaps he might like to use his hard-earned money to take the whole family to one of his favourite places, Center Parcs, he jumped at the chance. He became visibly more enthusiastic, and returned to the set the next day with renewed vigour. Paul and I were such proud parents as we watched him complete his scenes over the coming weeks. That's not to say we were not served an occasional wobbly: life cannot exist alongside Max without certain episodes peppering the day.

*

So here we are, sitting on the steps of the location house. The rest of the cast are inside, but when Max isn't needed for filming I try and make sure he stays out of the way. While Max's exuberance is undoubtedly infectious, at times it can be a little overwhelming and I'm keen that he doesn't hold things up for the production team.

Max seems so at home in this environment and for that reason I have tried to keep back and refrain from mothering him too much, partly because I think he behaves better when I'm not about, and partly because this is his world, not mine. I've shed all the initial anxieties I had at the start. The filming process, this world, has slotted naturally into our lives, Max's particularly. So I'm relaxed, preoccupied with doughnuts, but happy that my son is in the front room of the house with his mates, Judi, Cate and Bill. They are in the throes of completing a bohemian family dance scene: loud music filters out on to the street, and Max is in his element.

A good hour goes by, but eventually Max dashes out excitedly telling me that he's found a pussycat. He knows I love cats – we have three at home – so he's keen to drag me inside and show me his discovery. Plonked on the sofa in the living room is a big fat tabby.

Judi, also using the sofa for a well-earned rest, glances at the cat with amusement. 'He's certainly not part of the cast! He must come with the house; the family who normally live here must have left him behind.'

'Well, he certainly looks at home,' I reply.

You have to admire the sheer audacity of the animal; he looks at me as Max and I coo over him, giving him a scratch under his chin, as if to say, 'I have no idea why you people are here, but this is my house and nobody is going to stop me from enjoying my own sofa.' By now it's late afternoon, filming is always conducted at a furious pace and soon everyone will move on to the next scene. A lull is in the air as cast and crew pause for breath and enjoy a moment to relax. Max, aware that he might be finished for the day, seizes the opportunity to remind Martin of a promise he had made him earlier this morning.

Martin Harrison, the First Assistant Director, has a keen sense of how to 'work' Max. Apparently, there had been some negotiation between the two of them, so that when Max finished all his filming for the day, Martin would allow Max to continue to show off his dancing skills to the cast and crew. Max is not one to forget something like this, and true to his word, Martin set up the lounge and asks for a bit of hush. Max then declares that he wants his mum to dance with him. The thought of dancing in front of all these people is enough to bring me out in hives. 'No, not her, my other mum!' says Max.

In truth I have mixed feelings. I am terrifically relieved that I have just been let off the hook from an embarrassment of a lifetime, but I feel mortified that Max is demanding that Cate Blanchett, his mother in the film, dance with him. Cate is wonderful and rises to the occasion with elegance and charm. The two of them dance with abandonment as the cast and crew look on, cheering and clapping. Are they indulging my precocious son? You bet, and I love every one of them for it. I am quick to grab Max's hand once the music stops and whisk him away before his expanding ego gets the better of him. I wish I could have enjoyed the moment more and I find it hard to brush off my embarrassment. But Max has no such qualms; he has loved every minute of it, as he does life.

At the age of 13 my son has been forced to live with the relentless condition of Down's syndrome, and all that it inevitably throws at him. Yet through his own determination and tenacity, he's got to act in a Hollywood Movie, playing alongside the extraordinary talents of Judi Dench, Cate Blanchett and Bill Nighy.

In fact, less than a year later, Maggie Lunn is the casting director on Lynda La Plante's *Trial and Retribution XIII – Curriculum Vitae*, and has been asked by the director to get a 'kid who can really act' to play Miles Deacon, a boy who is a key witness in a thriller. This is a part not actually written for a boy with

Down's syndrome, just a boy with loads of talent. Another audition and Max's second screen role was soon secured.

So, now we have a Hollywood Movie star in our small family unit. Max fits the part perfectly, a true diva to the core. We are all delighted for him, as well as being a tad relieved. Max is a total extrovert. Given the choice and opportunity, Max would be out every night of the week living it up, bingo on a Monday, karaoke on a Tuesday, disco dancing on a Wednesday; you get the picture. As for Paul, Charlie and me, well next to him we're shy, retiring creatures who like nothing better than to stick our heads deep into a good book or knuckle down to surfing the net. That means things can get a bit taxing. We love Max dearly, but to have a gripping read punctuated by full, top of the lungs renditions of 'Old Bamboo', from *Chitty Chitty Bang Bang* or 'Money Money Money', from *Mamma Mia!*, is enough to test the patience of a saint.

To Max life is one big adventure: he chooses to see his cup as half full, positively overflowing, never half empty. Perhaps we could all learn a lesson from that.

9 October

*Charlie and Paul are off to watch the rugby at
Watford, so it's just me and Max today. I've said
he can pick what we do, anything, within reason. He
wants to go to Toys R Us to look at all the Dr Who
bits, and then go 'park cruising'. We trudge around
Toys R Us, with me practising my deep breathing.
My patience wins, and I manage to contain myself,
as we move from aisle to aisle examining everything.
He knows we're not there to buy and he is
tremendously good about not demanding anything.
I breathe a deep sigh of relief when, finally, he asks
to leave and we make our way back to the car. It's
now raining, which frankly deters neither of us,
especially not Max. He's elected to go 'park
cruising', and that is what we will do. Me, I'd rather
dip the tips of my fingers in burning candle wax.*

*Finally we arrive at park number three – Golders
Hill Park. After parking the car, we head straight for
the café. It's still raining heavily, so there are few
people about. Just Sunday dads and parents with
toddlers, who would otherwise be going stir crazy at
home.*

We queue for a cup of tea for me and an ice cream for Max; he cannot believe his luck. There are plenty of seats free, so we settle down by the window and watch the rain quench the lush green of the beautiful park. Scarcely a few minutes pass by before Max has finished his ice cream and is beaming with contentment. I ask him if it was as good as it looked and he reaches across the table and grabs my cheeks with both hands. He plants a big wet kiss smack on my lips and says, 'You're the best mum in the whole wide world, better than all the strawberry and all the vanilla ice cream.'

That's enough for me.

Life

A vulnerable baby protected by motherly love,
a heart crying out with uncontrollable demands,
perfectly content to be a cute little darling.

A nervous child is easy prey,
being introduced to life and lost in imagination,
wonderful toys to fill their hearts.

School children busy jamming their brains,
they'd rather be home,
at the critical point of their latest game.

Then will come the student,
having a crash with mates,
although supposed to be studying,
this is the life they enjoy,
still awaiting the surprises of adulthood.

Next comes a new family,
devoted partner and eager child,
awaiting the next holiday,
knowing there's work to be done.

Finally the elderly grandparent,
no job but a joyous family,
the support of a pension,
but they know the end is near.

This is life,
it may not be glorious but it's all we have,
so best make the most of it.

Charlie Lewis (age 11)